Fixing Post-Truth Politics

How the Republicans and Democrats Nominated Two Completely Unsuitable Candidates for President, and What the American Electorate Can Do About It Moving Forward

TOM MITSOFF

Dedication

This book is dedicated to my late father, **Chris Mitsoff**, who taught me how to write at a young age. His determined efforts to become published later in life inspired me in my own literary efforts …

and …

Alicia Dunams, whose Bestseller in a Weekend course[1] taught me how to write a book. I have purchased scores of educational materials online, and hers is without question the one which has taught me and benefitted me the most.

Preface

This book is written for the more than 100 million United States citizens who do not currently have a voice in national politics. These are the people in the political "middle," who, in effect, have no representation in the federal government. You will learn in this book that there are more "middle-grounders" than there are Democrats or Republicans in the U.S., but the "middle" has nobody standing up for it.

This book is written for the people in the middle who have an open mind and don't automatically subscribe and tie themselves to a position or statement just because one of the leaders of the Democratic or Republican parties says it.

You will read in this book how technological and cultural changes over the past half-century have led us to a point in our country's history where the truthfulness of presidential candidates' statements is not important to a substantial percentage of the electorate. This trend inspired Oxford Dictionaries to declare "post-truth" their word of the year for 2016. The term refers to a version of reporting and campaigning in which appealing to emotions is more important than factual accuracy.

This book is written for the more than 100 million people who cannot believe that our two major political parties nominated two such completely unsuitable candidates. This book will explain how and why it happened.

This book is also written for the more than 100 million people who can't believe what is happening to our nation's political culture, and who want to know what they can possibly do about it in the face of two dominant parties that are all about control and nothing else at this point. This book includes a plan to provide direction to these frustrated people who want to make a difference in our country before it becomes too late.

In the aftermath of the worst presidential campaign most people have ever seen, author Tom Mitsoff asked himself, "How did we possibly get to the point where we as a country nominated these two completely unsuitable candidates? And what can we do to change it?" His research and conclusions are reflected in the content presented in this book.

TABLE OF CONTENTS

Changes must happen

The office of President of the United States was respected and revered for most of the country's history. But in the past 40 years, an almost complete reversal has occurred. There is open disdain and disrespect for candidates for the office, and the people who eventually hold the position.

In 2016, the two major political parties nominated candidates completely unsuited for the office. By statute (the U.S. Constitution), they were qualified for consideration:

Age and Citizenship requirements - US Constitution, Article II, Section 1

No person except a natural born citizen, or a citizen of the United States, at the time of the adoption of this Constitution, shall be eligible to the office of President; neither shall any person be eligible to that office who shall not have attained to the age of thirty-five years, and been fourteen years a resident within the United States.

But in terms of personal integrity, Hillary Clinton and Donald Trump represented an all-time low in the quality of candidates presented to the U.S. electorate. One option was a person who knowingly accepted donations to her personal family foundation from figures of international influence in exchange for the opportunity to meet with, and hopefully influence decisions by, the U.S. Secretary of State. "Pay for play" was the term given to the practice, but a more accurate term is bribery.

The money then benefitted Hillary Clinton and her family directly. According to emails revealed by the WikiLeaks organization, the allegedly charitable Clinton Foundation paid for the multi-million-dollar wedding of Chelsea Clinton, and paid her living expenses for many years.

Hillary Clinton was the Secretary of State who thought it would be okay to run classified emails through a personal email server because it was more convenient for her personally. She also revealed that she viewed approximately half of the electorate as a "basket of deplorables. Right? Racist, sexist, homophobic, xenophobic, Islamophobic, you name it." (Technically, it was about a quarter of the electorate, because she said that half of Trump supporters belonged in that basket. But all Trump supporters certainly believed she was talking to them personally.)

Or, we had the choice of a man who bragged to friends on video about his success in grabbing women by the genitals because he is a celebrity, and about how he tried to have sex with a married woman. He also made fun of a reporter with arthrogryposis, a condition which limits the movement of joints. After referring to Serge Kovaleski as "a nice reporter" as a press conference, Trump began what appeared to be an impression of him, pointedly flopping his right arm around with his hand held at an odd angle. Consider this was someone Trump had known for years and had been interviewed by on several occasions.

Trump called ABC News reporter Tom Llamas "a sleaze" during a press conference, oddly adding "because you know the facts, and you know the facts well."

It was clear from a very early point of his campaign that Trump lacks any degree of decorum or respect for anybody who irritates him. His influence over people he views as subordinate to him comes from intimidating and bullying them. Certainly it has worked for him in the business world, but whether it will serve the United States of America well remains very much open to question.

Survey after survey showed that Clinton and Trump were the two most reviled presidential candidates in history. In state after state, people who went to the polls voted for so-called down-ticket races (such as Congress, governor and state legislative seats) but did not cast a vote for the presidential race.

In Michigan, about 88,000 people (approximately 2 percent of the electorate) submitted ballots without a vote for president. In New Hampshire, there were 6,200 more votes cast in the U.S. Senate race than for president. In Wisconsin, more people voted in a competitive U.S. Senate race than for president. Tens of thousands of voters across the country could not bring themselves to select any of the presidential candidates, even though they otherwise exercised their right to vote.

We will reveal in this book how we as a country and society got to a point where individuals as unsuited as Clinton and Trump emerged as the nominees of their respective parties. Polls conducted during the presidential campaign revealed that the U.S. population views the news media in an even more negative light than the candidates. There is a connection there, which we will also explore in this book.

The United States is at a critical point in its political and cultural history. Tensions are high for many reasons, not the least of which is the growth of minority demographics. In 2015, more minority babies were born in the U.S. than Caucasian babies. In 30 to 40 years, Caucasians will be less than 50 percent of the country's population. The U.S.A. will not have a racial majority, meaning that cultural clashes will continue and perhaps be even more pronounced. The country needs people of standout intelligence, leadership, and integrity to be willing to lead our nation. But those people are not volunteering for the job, once considered the most illustrious and prestigious in the country. Why not? We'll examine that point as well.

You'll read two main sections of this book:

- The history and perfect storm of cultural changes that led up to the 2016 presidential election season; and

- What we as a society must do to increase the quality of candidates presented to us on our general election ballots.

Changes must happen. The United States electorate must not allow the choice of president in 2020 to be between such unqualified individuals. We must strive for the standard of nominating the cream of the crop, who are the best of what our country has to offer. The intent of this book is to begin the discussion of how we as an electorate and a society make that happen.

'This is the way they'll be elected forevermore'

Innovation and changes in cultural norms influence United States presidential elections. In the 21st century, we take for granted that information flows at us from all directions on a constant basis. Remember that it hasn't always been that way.

What did voters use for a source of information on candidates in the first half of the 20th century? Word of mouth and newspapers, which were at their absolute peak of influence and consumption.

Before Trump's win, the biggest upset in U.S. presidential election history was incumbent Democrat Harry S. Truman defeating Republican challenger Thomas Dewey, governor of New York, in 1948. There are many parallels between the two races. Truman, who succeeded Franklin D. Roosevelt after his death in 1945, was behind in the public polling throughout the election. His Democratic party had a three-way ideological split, with both the far right of the party (Dixiecrat Strom Thurmond) and far left (Henry A. Wallace of the Progressive Party) running third-party campaigns.

Dewey and his advisors were so convinced that a win was imminent that they believed all they had to do was to avoid major mistakes. Dewey carefully avoided risks, avoided controversial issues, and was vague on what he planned to do as president. Non-political assertions of the obvious filled most of his speeches, including the now-infamous quote, "You know that your future is still ahead of you."

Truman responded with a slashing, no-holds-barred campaign. He ridiculed Dewey by name and criticized Dewey's refusal to address specific issues. Truman nicknamed the Republican-controlled Congress the "do-nothing" Congress, a bit of foreshadowing of President Obama's political strategy. Truman's remark prompted criticism from Republican Congressional leaders, but no comment from Dewey. In fact, Dewey rarely mentioned Truman's name during the campaign, which fit into his strategy of appearing to be above petty partisan politics.

Movie theaters agreed to play newsreel-like campaign films supporting the two major-party candidates in the final weeks of the campaign. Each campaign organization created a short feature.

The Dewey film had very high production values in part because it was shot professionally on a large budget. It reinforced a perception of the New York governor as distant and cautious.

(See the Dewey film at http://fixposttruthpolitics.com/the-thomas-dewey-story/)

The Truman film relied heavily on public-domain and newsreel footage of the president taking part in major world events and signing important legislation. The always cash-strapped Truman campaign hastily produced the film on virtually no budget.

(See the Truman film at http://fixposttruthpolitics.com/the-harry-s-truman-story/)

Perhaps unintentionally, the Truman film visually reinforced an image of him as engaged and decisive. Years later, historian David McCullough cited the expensive, but lackluster, Dewey film, and the far cheaper, but more effective, Truman film, as important factors in determining the preferences of undecided voters.

It was the first case of the visual media playing an important role in swinging the sentiments of the electorate, which returned Truman to office despite the Chicago Daily Tribune's ill-fated banner headline, "DEWEY DEFEATS TRUMAN." (The newspaper was so sure of Dewey's victory that on Tuesday afternoon before any polls closed, it printed the headline for the following day.)

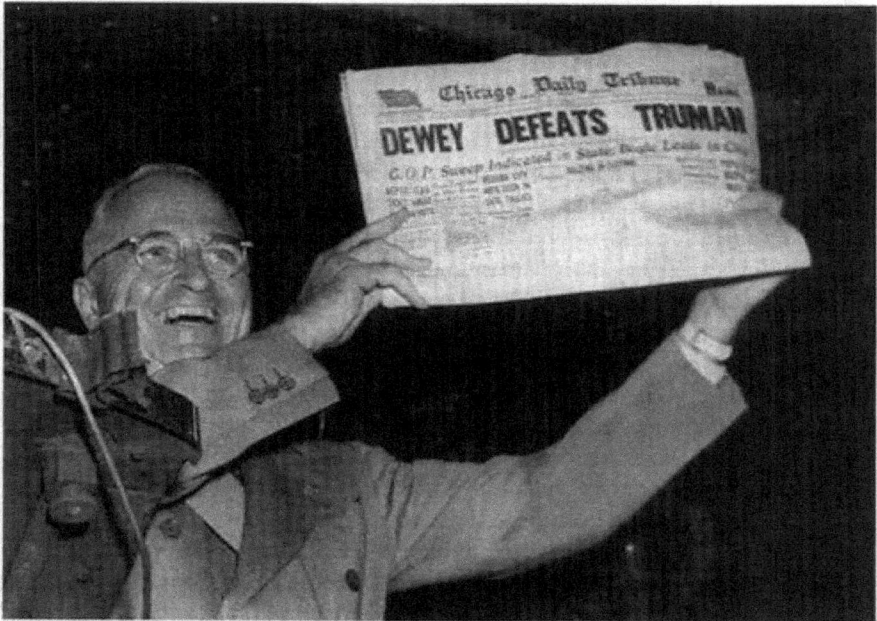

Part of the reason Truman's victory came as such a shock was because of flaws in the then-emerging craft of public opinion polling. As the 1948 campaign entered its final days, polls showed Truman gaining. Though Truman lost all nine of the Gallup Poll's post-convention surveys, Dewey's polling lead continued to shrink — from 17 points in late September to nine points in mid-October to just five points by the end of the month, a number just above the poll's margin of error. Most political analysts were reticent to break with the conventional wisdom and say that a Truman victory was a serious possibility despite the incumbent's momentum.

Pollster Elmo Roper said on September 9, nearly two months before election day, "Thomas E. Dewey is almost as good as elected," adding that he didn't want to act like a sports announcer pretending he is witnessing a very tight race. Roper did not poll voters again until the final week before the election. That poll showed a small shift to Truman. But Dewey still had a big lead, so Roper decided not to recant his previous position.

The expectation of a Dewey victory was so pervasive that most media and political pundits had articles pre-written for publication the day after Election Day. Life magazine published a large photo in its final edition before the election titled, "Our Next President Rides by Ferryboat over San Francisco Bay." Dewey and his staff were pictured riding across the city's harbor. Newsweek magazine polled 50 experts; all 50 predicted a Dewey win.

Nationally syndicated columnist Drew Pearson wrote before the election that Truman's election was "impossible."

Commentator Walter Winchell reported that gambling odds were 15 to 1 against Truman. More than 500 newspapers, representing more than 78 percent of the nation's total daily circulation, endorsed Dewey. Truman received 182 endorsements, accounting for just 10 percent of America's newspaper readership, being surpassed by Thurmond, who got the remaining 12 percent from mostly Southern newspapers.

On Election Day, Alistair Cooke, the distinguished writer for the Manchester Guardian newspaper in the United Kingdom, published an article titled "Harry S. Truman: A Study of a Failure." NBC News constructed a large cardboard model of the White House with two elephants that would pop out when the network's newscasters announced Dewey's victory. NBC didn't place donkeys in the White House model because Truman's defeat was considered such a certainty.

Truman went to his hometown of Independence, Missouri, near Kansas City, on Election Night to await the returns. The outcome seemed so presumptive that some of his aides had already accepted other jobs. None of the reporters traveling on his campaign train believed he would win. Meanwhile, Dewey, his family, and campaign staff gathered at the Roosevelt Hotel in New York City to await the returns.

As the results came in, Truman took an early lead that he never lost. Leading radio commentators, such as H. V. Kaltenborn of NBC, maintained their belief in the pre-election mindset. Kaltenborn confidently predicted that Dewey would overcome Truman and win once the "late returns" came in.

Truman awoke at midnight and turned on the radio in his room. He heard Kaltenborn say that while Truman was still ahead in the popular vote, he could not possibly win. Truman awoke again at 4 a.m. and heard on the radio that his popular-vote lead was now nearly two million votes. For the rest of his life, Truman gleefully mimicked Kaltenborn's ostentatious voice predicting his loss throughout that election night.

Dewey, meanwhile, knew he was in trouble when early returns from New England and New York had him running well behind his anticipated vote total. He stayed awake for the rest of the night and early morning checking the results as they came in. By 10:30 a.m., it was clear Dewey had lost. At 11:14 a.m., he sent a telegram of concession to Truman.

Television? It existed, but it was still in its infancy. There were around 500,000 television sets and only 41 television stations on the air across the country in 1948. Most of them were in major metropolitan areas such as New York, Chicago, Boston and Los Angeles. TVs were exceptionally rare in the nation's 40.5 million households, and especially so in rural areas. Many of the TVs in existence were in bars, used as an incentive to bring customers back.

1948 General Electric television (on display in the Museum of Science and Industry in Chicago)

By the 1952 presidential election, the political parties were aware of the potential of the new medium. The Republican Campaign Manual for 1952 said:

> Television and radio are assuming increasing importance in every political campaign and no campaign manager can afford to overlook their value in bringing the Republican Party's message into the voter's homes. The extra effort and skill they require pay off at the ballot box.

Chairman Leonard Hall of the Republican National Committee told the National Federation of Republican Women in Washington on March 1: "We must choose able and personable candidates who can 'sell themselves' because TV has changed the course of campaigns." Hall added that television had destroyed the power of special interests to deliver blocs of votes because elections now were being won in the living rooms of individual voters.

The Democratic National Committee's handbook for candidates, A Campaign Guide to Political Publicity, referred to television as a "spectacular weapon," possibly "your most important campaign tool." It reminded candidates that in five minutes they could "visit more families in their living rooms" than could be seen "in a month of personal calls." Television offered the unknown contender "the quickest route to becoming a live flesh-and-blood personality in the minds of the voters."

Candidates were urged not only to buy video time but also to seek guest appearances on non-political programs. The Republican manual noted that free appearances "ease the burden on the party organization's hard-pressed treasury," and "enable the candidate to get his message across to established program audiences, many of whom might be reluctant to listen to straight political programs."

By mid-1952, more than 18 million television sets were in American homes, and 112 telecasting stations were in operation in 66 market areas. Studies indicated that three significant segments of the electorate could be reached by television: big-city, medium-sized county, and rural voters. Surveys disclosed that around 70 million persons watched some parts of the telecasts of the two nominating conventions.

During the 1954 congressional campaign, Newsweek reported: "Campaign managers the country over were asking themselves that fateful question: 'How does he project?' more often than they were worrying over their candidates' voting records or hand-shaking ability....Today's politician is now convinced that one picture is worth 10,000 of radio's words."

President Dwight D. Eisenhower, speaking informally to the National Association of Radio and Television Broadcasters on May 25, 1955, mentioned broadcasting's growing power "in swaying public opinion." He called radio and television "a mighty force in our civilization, one that is certain to grow ... and be more powerful in its influence upon all of us." He proved to be prescient, and it didn't take long for his words to ring true.

The 1960 presidential election, pitting Democrat John F. Kennedy against Eisenhower's vice president, Richard Nixon, was the first in which the influence of television was a deciding factor in the race.

In August, most polls showed Nixon with a slim lead over Kennedy, and many political prognosticators regarded him as the favorite to win. However, Nixon experienced bad luck throughout the fall campaign. Eisenhower, who had long been ambivalent about Nixon, held a televised press conference during which reporter Charles Mohr of Time magazine mentioned Nixon's claims that he had been a valuable administration insider and adviser. The reporter asked Eisenhower if he could give an example of an idea of Nixon's that he had heeded. Eisenhower replied with the flip comment, "If you give me a week, I might think of one."

Although both Eisenhower and Nixon later claimed the president was merely joking with the reporter, the remark hurt Nixon. It undercut his claims of having more decision-making experience than Kennedy. The comment proved so damaging to Nixon that the Democrats turned Eisenhower's statement into a television commercial:

> Every Republican politician wants you to believe that Richard Nixon is, quote, "experienced." They even want you to believe that he has actually been making decisions in the White House. But listen to the man who should know best, the President of the United States. A reporter recently asked President Eisenhower this question about Nixon's experience.
>
> "I just wondered if you could give us an example of a major idea of his that you had

adopted in that role as the decider and final...”

“If you give me a week, I might think of one. I don't remember.” (laughs)

At the same press conference, President Eisenhower said, “No one can make a decision except me.”

And as for any major ideas from Mr. Nixon, “If you give me a week, I might think of one. I don't remember.”

President Eisenhower could not remember, but the voters will remember. For real leadership in the 60's, help elect Senator John F. Kennedy for President.

(Watch the commercial at
http://fixposttruthpolitics.com/attack-ad/)

That was one of the first television "attack" ads, which today are the clear majority of political advertising. But the turning point of the campaign came with the four Kennedy-Nixon debates, the first presidential debates ever. They were also the first held on television and thus attracted enormous attention. By this point, approximately 90 percent of U.S. homes had a television, and an estimated 70 million people watched the first debate.

Nixon made campaign stops until just a few hours before the first debate started. He had bashed his knee on a car door while campaigning in North Carolina a few weeks earlier and developed an infection that landed him in the hospital. He emerged two weeks later frail and 20 pounds underweight, but immediately resumed an intense whistle-stop campaign.

Stepping out of the car upon arrival at the debate in Chicago, Nixon banged his bad knee again and exacerbated his injury, adding to the effects of a grueling day on the campaign trail. In modern-day politics, candidates make sure they are well-rested and prepared for debates. Not realizing what impact television would have, Nixon opted for the day of in-person campaign stops rather than rest and preparation.

While answering questions, Nixon looked off to the side (and not directly into the camera) to address the various reporters. Television viewers perceived it as shifting his gaze to avoid eye contact with the public – damaging for a man already known derisively as "Tricky Dick." Kennedy, on the other hand, stared directly into the camera as he answered each question, as though he was talking directly to the voters instead of the reporters.

Nixon also refused makeup for the first debate, and his beard stubble showed prominently on the era's black-and-white TV screens. Both candidates had rejected the offer for makeup artists. At his aides' urging, Nixon agreed to apply a coat of Lazy Shave, a drugstore pancake makeup he had used on previous occasions to mask his five o'clock shadow. But when he started sweating under the hot studio lights, the powder seemed to melt off Nixon's face, giving way to visible beads of perspiration.

Chicago Mayor Richard J. Daley, after seeing Nixon on the debate telecast, reportedly said, "My God, they've embalmed him before he even died." In the following day's edition, the *Chicago Daily News* ran the headline, "Was Nixon Sabotaged by TV Makeup Artists?"

Nixon appeared so poorly on television in the first debate that his mother called him afterward to ask if he was sick. Kennedy, on the other hand, rested and prepared extensively beforehand, appearing tanned, confident, and relaxed during the debate. He had spent time in Florida before the debate, so though he declined makeup, his skin was tanned.

People who watched the debate on TV overwhelmingly believed Kennedy had won, while radio listeners (a smaller audience) thought Nixon was the victor.

After the first debate, polls had Kennedy moving from a slight deficit into a slight lead. In the three remaining debates, Nixon regained the weight he had lost, wore television makeup, and seemed more forceful than in the first debate.

However, up to 20 million fewer viewers watched the remaining debates than the first. Political observers felt that Kennedy won the first debate, Nixon took the second and third debates, while the fourth debate, seen as the strongest performance by both men, was a draw.

No one realized just how much TV mattered for candidates until after those 1960 debates. Up to that point, politics had not played out on television, because TV was primarily an entertainment medium. People didn't consider it a source of serious and pertinent information.

The next televised presidential debate wouldn't take place for 16 years, primarily because candidates became wary of their influence. Lyndon B. Johnson was too intimidated by television to debate Barry Goldwater in 1964. Having been burned before, Nixon declined to debate Hubert Humphrey on TV in 1968 and George McGovern in 1972. Televised debates were back in 1976 when incumbent President Gerald Ford took on his Democratic challenger, Jimmy Carter.

They've been standard practice in each presidential campaign since.

Before the Kennedy presidency, television was way behind print journalism in terms of resources American audiences relied upon for news. But it wasn't long before people relied on TV news for the day's headlines as well as updates on American troops in Vietnam, notably the numbers of soldiers killed or wounded.

When something major occurred on TV, the whole country could watch it together. TV news was the opposite of entertainment TV. The civil rights era, the JFK assassination and the space race all unfolded on TV. As NBC News anchor David Brinkley stated, "Television showed the American people TO the American people."

When Nixon ran for president again in 1968, he made a cameo appearance on the popular comedy show "Rowan & Martin's Laugh-In," uttering the show's famous catchphrase, "Sock it to me."

(Watch it at http://fixposttruthpolitics.com/sock-it-to-me/)

It was the first appearance for a presidential candidate on a comedy show. For the rest of his life, Nixon was steadfast in the belief that his appearance on "Laugh-In" won him the 1968 election. While TV arguably lost Nixon the election once, it may very well have earned him the victory the second time around.

More importantly, the perception of how Richard Nixon's Laugh-In appearance shaped the 1968 election changed the world of politics. A team of media handlers — including the future president of Fox News, Roger Ailes — worked to reshape the image of Nixon from that of a bore uncomfortable in his own skin to someone larger than life, almost legendary in nature. It was the dawn of the era of the political candidate as a product to be marketed to consumers who care more about personality and style than issues and substance.

There once was a time when politicians, Nixon initially being one of them, felt sincerity was a virtue. But it was soon realized that clutching to such a concept in the television age was a political death knell. It was manipulation of the media — the message — that was most important. One week before the 1968 election of Richard Nixon, Ailes would say, "This is the beginning of a whole new concept. This is it. This is the way they'll be elected forevermore."[2]

The end of reverence for presidents

On June 17, 1972, police arrested five men milling around the sixth floor of the Watergate Hotel in Washington, D.C. in the wee hours of the morning. The next day authorities described the incident as an elaborate plot to bug the offices of the Democratic National Committee.

Little did anyone know at the time that the foiled break-in at the Watergate hotel would lead to the downfall of a president, convictions of 30 of his advisors and staff members, and a change in the national attitude toward its elected leaders.

Plain-clothes officers of the Washington Police Department walked in on the five men at 2:30 a.m. Two ceiling panels were removed in the office of the secretary of the Democratic Party. The secretary's office was adjacent to the office of Democratic National Chairman Lawrence F. O'Brien, and the men were allegedly in the process of installing bugging devices which would have picked up conversations and phone calls in O'Brien's office. Much later, investigators learned that they were there to repair and replace some bugs they had already installed in a previous break-in.

With four of the five burglars being residents of Miami, Fla., rather than Washington, and the fifth being a former CIA employee, the red flags went up immediately that there was something terribly amiss. Two of the Washington Post reporters who covered the story of the five men's arrests — Bob Woodward and Carl Bernstein — followed their instincts and soon began to uncover a paper and money trail that connected the Watergate burglars with President Richard Nixon's re-election committee.

Nixon's fate was sealed when the Senate convened public hearings on the Watergate matter. Senators learned that the president had installed a sophisticated tape-recording system in the Oval Office which recorded every conversation held there. Nixon and his aides sparred with the Senate committee and the independent Watergate prosecutor over whether he had to surrender the tapes. In a scenario similar to Bill Clinton's denials and eventual grand jury testimony in the Monica Lewinsky scandal, Nixon kept bobbing and weaving in an attempt to avoid the knockout punch the prosecutor was trying to deliver.

Eventually, with the country in turmoil and Nixon ready to be served with articles of impeachment — meaning that the Senate could have tried him — he finally resigned on August 8, 1974, more than two years after the break-in that was the actual beginning of the end.

Nixon was popular enough to have won re-election by landslide in 1972, so he wasn't in any real political trouble. He didn't need to dig up any dirt on the Democrats, but he didn't realize that. He was insecure enough to think he had to eliminate any shred of hope the Democrats would have. Nixon certainly would have won without the political "dirty tricks" perpetrated on his behalf. The whole sequence of events was a great American tragedy.

Its most lasting effect is the changed way we look at our elected leaders. Most Americans, before Watergate, viewed their president with reverence. Presidential policies and decisions were questioned in a respectful manner (with the possible exception of Vietnam war era protests).

It was a seismic shock to our culture – and our media – that a president would do something unconstitutional and criminal to ensure his re-election. Joe and Jane Q. Public never imagined this possibility. They understood that presidents made decisions based on information given to them by their staffs and that sometimes those decisions could be swayed by personal beliefs, opinions, and even hunches.

But when Richard Nixon said during a November 17, 1973, press conference, "People have got to know whether or not their president is a crook. Well, I'm not a crook," he was lying.

(Watch it at http://fixposttruthpolitics.com/i-am-not-a-crook/)

The breaking and entering at Watergate had its origins in June 1971, when the first excerpt of the "Pentagon Papers" was published in the *New York Times*. RAND Corporation employee and anti-war activist Daniel Ellsberg leaked confidential and politically explosive Defense Department documents about the Vietnam War to the press.

The documents were more damaging to Lyndon Johnson and John F. Kennedy than Nixon, but being blindsided on a matter of national security embarrassed Nixon. He was concerned that maybe others who sided with Ellsberg who were gaining access to other secrets of the administration.

Nixon and staffers John Mitchell, Bob Haldeman, John Ehrlichman and Chuck Colson, began putting together a plan to deal with Ellsberg and anyone else who might be planning similar actions. They created a secret office within the White House called the "Plumbers," including two right-wing espionage "experts" named E. Howard Hunt and G. Gordon Liddy. Hunt was a former CIA operative, and Liddy was a retired attorney who would later go on to some degree of media fame on conservative-oriented radio and TV.

The two were instructed to dig up whatever they could on Ellsberg, and they discovered that he regularly saw a psychiatrist. The two broke into the psychiatrist's office and read through his medical files, hoping to find information with which to embarrass Ellsberg.

The broad rationale for the Plumbers' activities seemed to be that since Nixon's enemies were breaking the law and getting away with it, Nixon's team would also need to break the law to keep pace with their enemies. Nixon and his staff worked to quickly develop a private espionage capability since they were sure enemies surrounded them.

Ellsberg was charged under the Espionage Act of 1917 along with other charges of theft and conspiracy, carrying a total maximum sentence of 115 years. However, Judge William Matthew Byrne dismissed all charges on May 11, 1973, due to governmental misconduct and illegal evidence gathering.

In July 1974, the House Judiciary Committee passed the first of three articles of impeachment against Nixon, charging obstruction of justice. With a post-impeachment conviction likely, Nixon resigned as president on August 9, 1974. Gerald

Ford, whom Nixon had appointed vice president in 1973 after Spiro Agnew resigned his office amid charges of bribery, extortion and tax evasion during his tenure as governor of Maryland, succeeded him. President Ford then pardoned Nixon on September 8, 1974.

Reporters Woodward and Bernstein became national celebrities and heroes for the investigative journalism work they did that brought the truth to light. People of all ages who wanted to make a difference turned to careers in journalism. The best and brightest went to work doing what the Constitution intended a free press to do – perform a watchdog function over government on behalf of the citizenry.

This new wave of journalists — along with their veteran predecessors — became much more aggressive. In a trend that began in the wake of Watergate, the media is now much more aggressive in its questioning of our presidents and attempting to uncover all possible pertinent information about them, including personal. As a result, presidents now keep their distance from the media in every way imaginable. Handlers painstakingly choreograph all public appearances and speeches to keep unexpected questions at an absolute minimum. And that has only deepened the mistrust and even disrespect between media and politicians.

Ford bore much of the anger and scrutiny from both the media and the American public in Nixon's wake. Following the ultra-controversial Nixon pardon, Saigon — the capital of South Vietnam — fell shortly thereafter, effectively ending the Vietnam War as Americans literally fled the U.S. embassy via airlift. The economy was in recession, and Ford took a tumble down the stairs of Air Force One while in Austria, leading to the moniker, "Klutz in Chief."

One example of the change in the level of respect for presidents and the office was on the at-the-time-new comedy show Saturday Night Live. On Nov. 8, 1975, Chevy Chase debuted his impersonation of the bumbling Gerald Ford. In what became a recurring sketch, Chase portrayed Ford as a clumsy oaf who might mistake a water glass for a telephone, go tumbling over his desk or take a misstep completely off the stage.

Ford's press secretary Ron Nessen and the president tested the waters by inviting Chevy Chase to perform at a White House dinner in March of 1976. To the audience's surprise, the president emerged as the star of the show. He reminded the comedian that "I'm Gerald Ford, and you're not." With the primary race heating up and campaign budgets reaching pre-convention limits, Ford welcomed the free publicity the evening generated. He pledged to send Nessen to Chase's show in return.

Al Franken, then a writer for SNL, invited Nessen to guest host during the New Hampshire primary. On April 17, 1976, along with Nessen serving as SNL guest host, Ford uttered the famous line: "Live from New York, it's Saturday night!" Pre-recorded in the Oval Office, the president's introduction served as his blessing to Nessen's appearance. But it would become a controversial evening.[3]

In one sketch, Nessen played himself, opposite Chevy Chase's impression of the president, and he explained his rationale for hosting.

"And that's why I want to host this show, to demonstrate that this administration has a sense of humor," he told the fake Ford. "You may remember in 1968, Nixon said, 'Sock it to me' on Laugh-In, and it may have made the difference in the election."

Reviews of the show were not kind to Nessen. Many critics felt the press secretary had made a "gross error of judgment" by appearing on a show that lacked the "dignity" of the Oval Office. It didn't make a difference at election time, either, when Jimmy Carter successfully took the White House from the incumbent Ford.

Ford and Nessen may have lost the election, but Nessen's SNL sketch had unintended though lasting legacies for the office of the president. It contributed to the growing perception that being entertaining was necessary to succeed politically, and further transformed entertainment forums into political battlefields. This belief has since become a reality of modern politics, a conviction further reinforced by the growing place of entertainers, consultants and "spin doctors" in campaigns.

Ford's attempt to "humanize" the presidency with humor made modern presidents more relatable but, ironically, less accessible. While candidates still shake hands in key primary states, entertainment is the filter through which many Americans meet the nation's most important politicians. The election of a reality television star with no support from the mainstream establishment of the party in November 2016 makes that point very clear.

Presidents used to be our version of royalty. Now they're viewed by most people as necessary evils who serve in spite of their many taints.

Something else happening in the 1970s would be every bit as important in the way we view candidates and politics as

Watergate and its aftermath. Cable television was becoming available in a growing portion of the country. Most households at the time received maybe four or five local over-the-air channels, tops, through their TV antennas. The further away from an urban area a home was, the better chance that the family's TV reception would be fuzzy and intermittent.

As far back as 1948, cable television was delivering programming to communities in Arkansas, Oregon, and Pennsylvania that could not receive broadcast signals. "Community antennas" were erected on mountain tops or other high points, and homes were connected to the antenna towers via cable to receive the broadcast signals.

By 1962, almost 800 cable systems serving 850,000 subscribers were in business. Well-known corporate names like Westinghouse, TelePrompTer, and Cox began investing in the business. They joined early entrepreneurs like Bill Daniels, Martin Malarkey and Jack Kent Cooke in the cable TV game.[4]

Local television stations viewed the growth of cable through importing distant signals as competition. The Federal Communications Commission (FCC) responded to the broadcast industry's concerns and expanded its jurisdiction, placing restrictions on the ability of cable systems to import distant television signals. The restrictions created a "freeze" effect on the development of cable systems in major markets, lasting into the early 1970s. The FCC also limited the ability of cable operators to offer movies, sporting events, and syndicated programming.

The freeze on cable's development lasted until 1972, when a policy of gradual cable deregulation led to, among other things, modified restrictions on the importation of distant signals. The clamp on growth had adverse financial effects, especially on access to capital. Money for cable growth and expansion all but dried up for several years.

However, concerted industry efforts at the federal, state, and local levels resulted in the continued lessening of restrictions on cable throughout the decade. These changes, coupled with cable's pioneering of satellite communications technology, led to a pronounced growth of services to consumers and a substantial increase in cable subscribers.

In 1972, Charles Dolan and Gerald Levin of Sterling Manhattan Cable launched the nation's first pay-TV network, Home Box Office (HBO). This venture led to the creation of a national satellite distribution system that used a newly approved domestic satellite transmission.[5] Satellites changed the business dramatically, paving the way for the explosive growth of program networks.

The second service to use the satellite was a local television station in Atlanta that primarily broadcast sports and classic movies. The station, owned by R.E. "Ted" Turner, was distributed by satellite to cable systems nationwide, and soon became known as the first "superstation," WTBS.

By the end of the decade, growth had resumed, and nearly 16 million households were cable subscribers.

Ted Turner and 25 other investors founded Cable News Network (CNN) in 1980 at the cost of $20 million. Upon its launch, CNN became the first channel to provide 24-hour television news coverage and was the first all-news television network in the United States.

The network launched on Sunday, June 1, 1980, at 5 p.m. Eastern Time with an original staff of 25 employees based at its headquarters in Atlanta, and bureaus in Chicago, Dallas, Los Angeles, New York City, San Francisco and Washington, D.C. The inaugural broadcast on the channel was an introduction by Turner, who announced:

> We won't be signing off until the world ends. We'll be on, we'll be covering it live, and that will be our last, last event. We'll play the national anthem for one time on the first of June, and that's all. When the end of the world comes, we'll play 'Nearer My God to Thee' before we sign off.

The husband and wife team of Dave Walker and Lois Hart anchored the channel's first newscast following the introduction and a pre-recorded version of "The Star-Spangled Banner" (which was a tradition whenever a new Turner-owned network launched) that was played afterward, Among the first segments was an interview with then-President Jimmy Carter by Daniel Schorr.

On January 1, 1982, the channel launched a spin-off network called CNN2, which was subsequently renamed Headline News (HLN) the following year in January 1983. Whereas CNN featured a mix of newscasts and specialized topical and feature programs, Headline News was originally formatted to strictly focus on rolling news coverage. Headline News featured half-hour newscasts 24 hours a day with segments scheduled in fixed time slots each half-hour. It was one of the first news channels to utilize a "wheel" schedule. Headline

News would scale back its rolling news coverage in February 2005, with the incorporation of personality-based news discussion programs during its nighttime schedule.

Following the launch of CNN, other cable news channels launched in an attempt to capitalize on the channel's growing success. One of the first was Satellite News Channel, which launched on June 21, 1982 with a mix of national and regionally focused newscasts; after the channel had ceased operations on October 27, 1983, its satellite transponder slot was subsequently purchased by Turner to expand the distribution of Headline News further into additional homes.

Along with around-the-clock news coverage, CNN initiated the idea of recurring news analysis and discussion shows with hosts who would become well-known personalities. Among the early programs on CNN were:

- "Moneyline" premiered in 1980 and was CNN's main financial program for more than 20 years. As the show, hosted by Lou Dobbs, moved more towards general news and economic and political commentary, it was renamed "Moneyline with Lou Dobbs," "Lou Dobbs Moneyline" and then "Lou Dobbs Tonight." In 2010, Dobbs – the last remaining original host from the network's launch in 1980 – resigned amid controversy over his questioning of whether President Barack Obama was a native-born U.S. citizen – a qualification for the presidency required under the U.S. Constitution.
- "Evans & Novak," with Rowland Evans and Robert Novak as its hosts, became one of the cable network's most-watched discussion programs. Shortly thereafter, Al Hunt and Mark Shields joined the show as occasional panelists; the name of the program was eventually changed to "Evans, Novak, Hunt &

Shields" in 1998 when Hunt and Shields became permanent members of the show.

- "Crossfire," a late-night political debate program, was hosted by liberal Tom Braden and conservative Pat Buchanan. The idea of the program came about when Braden and Buchanan debated on a daily radio show in 1978. The show soon became popular and was moved to a primetime slot.

- "Larry King Live," a primetime interview show, featured interviews with one or more prominent individuals, mainly celebrities, politicians and businesspeople. The show became the longest-running program on CNN, lasting for 25 years until King's retirement from the network in 2010.

Those programs were the precursors for what is now nightly viewing on all the news-oriented cable television networks.

Along with the new programming, CNN became known for being the source for live coverage of breaking news through these events:

- On January 28, 1986, CNN was the only TV network to provide live coverage of the launch of the Space Shuttle Challenger to the public. However, NASA TV provided the live coverage to schools nationwide. The Space Shuttle Challenger abruptly disintegrated just 73 seconds after lift-off. Seven astronauts, including schoolteacher Christa McAuliffe, were killed in the disaster.

- On October 14, 1987, 18-month-old toddler Jessica McClure fell down a well in Midland, Texas. CNN quickly reported on the story, and the event helped make its name.

- The first Persian Gulf War in 1991 was a watershed event for CNN that catapulted the network past the "big three" American networks for the first time in its history, largely due to an unprecedented, historical scoop: CNN was the only news outlet with the ability to communicate from inside Iraq during the initial hours of the American bombing campaign, with live reports from the al-Rashid Hotel in Baghdad by reporters Bernard Shaw, John Holliman, and Peter Arnett.

The moment when bombing began was announced on CNN by Bernard Shaw on January 16, 1991 as follows:[6]

> This is Bernie Shaw. Something is happening outside. ... Peter Arnett, join me here. Let's describe to our viewers what we're seeing ... The skies over Baghdad have been illuminated. ... We're seeing bright flashes going off all over the sky.

The live coverage was picked up by stations and networks throughout the U.S. and beyond, with some estimating that around 1 billion people watched around the globe. It was the first live coverage of an unfolding war from the scene.

In 1996, CNN received its first major competitors with the launch of MSNBC, originally a joint venture between NBC and Microsoft, and News Corporation's Fox News Channel. The three rival networks now battle for market share in the cable news market.

The 1984 Cable Act established a more favorable regulatory framework for the industry, stimulating investment in cable plant and programming on an unprecedented level.

Deregulation provided by the 1984 Act had a strong positive effect on the rapid growth of cable services. From 1984 through 1992, the industry spent more than $15 billion on the wiring of America, and billions more on program development, the largest private construction project since World War II.

Satellite delivery, combined with the federal government's relaxation of cable's restrictive regulatory structure, allowed the cable industry to become a major force in providing high-quality video entertainment and information to consumers. By the end of the decade, nearly 53 million households subscribed to cable, and cable program networks had increased from 28 in 1980 to 79 by 1989.[7] Some of this growth, however, was accompanied by rising prices for consumers, incurring growing concern among policy makers.

In 1992, Congress responded to cable price increases and other market factors with legislation that once again hampered cable growth and opened heretofore "exclusive" cable programming to other competitive distribution technologies such as "wireless cable" and the emerging direct satellite broadcast (DBS) business.

In spite of the effect of the '92 Act, the number of satellite networks continued their explosive growth, based largely on the alternative idea of targeting programming to a specific "niche" audience. By the end of 1995, there were 139 cable programming services available nationwide, in addition to many regional programming networks. By the spring of 1998, the number of national cable video networks had grown to 171.

By that time, the average subscriber could choose from a wide selection of quality programming, with more than 57 percent of all subscribers receiving at least 54 channels, up from 47 in 1996. And at the end of the decade, approximately 7 in 10 television households, more than 65 million, had opted to subscribe to cable.

Also during the latter half of the decade, cable operating companies commenced a major upgrade of their distribution networks, investing $65 billion between 1996 and 2002 to build higher capacity hybrid networks of fiber optic and coaxial cable.[8] These "broadband" networks provide multichannel video, two-way voice, high-speed Internet access, and high definition and advanced digital video services all on a single wire into the home.

The upgrade to broadband networks enabled cable companies to introduce high-speed Internet access to customers in the mid-90s, and competitive local telephone and digital cable services later in the decade.

Along with the massive increase of consumption of news networks via cable television, another newcomer to the national scene changed the way the public and the media viewed the presidency and politics in general.

Rush Limbaugh began his radio talk show — in its familiar format of political commentary and listener calls — in 1984 at Sacramento, California radio station KFBK. In 1988, Limbaugh began broadcasting his show nationally from radio station WABC in New York City. In 2014, the show's flagship station became WOR, also in New York. But he does The Rush Limbaugh Show via remote live from his home area of Palm Beach, Florida.

When the Republican Party won control of Congress in the 1994 midterm elections, the freshman Republican class awarded Limbaugh an honorary membership in their caucus, due to the influence his conservative opinions were having on the national political scene. This confirmed Limbaugh as an influential figure nationally.

President Bill Clinton's second term was when Limbaugh's attacks, and national ratings, exploded. There were many Clinton policies and actions that Limbaugh lampooned and openly criticized daily. But the one that changed everything was the revelation by the Drudge Report on January 17, 1998, that Clinton had sexual relations with an intern in the White House.[9] It was just another in a sequence of reports alleging inappropriate and even borderline criminal acts by Clinton toward several women.

The tone of Limbaugh's daily attacks was pointed and gave credence to reporting by sources outside the mainstream media. Clinton was impeached in 1999 when the sexual relations with the intern became commingled with other cases in which the Clintons were under investigation.

Special Prosecutor Kenneth Starr's investigation initially focused on a 1994 lawsuit in which former Arkansas state employee Paula Jones alleged Clinton had requested sexual favors from him. In a deposition for that case, investigators questioned Clinton about his relations with several women, including Lewinsky. In that under-oath deposition, he denied having sexual relations with the intern (which of course, he later acknowledged).

Clinton's impeachment trial in the Senate from January 7 through February 12, 1999, focused primarily on the fact that he lied under oath. Fifty senators voted that he was guilty of obstructing, and 45 said he was guilty of perjury. But the two-thirds majority of senators needed for conviction and removal from office was not reached.

Nevertheless, Limbaugh's influence reached its peak at that moment. He could create political stars, sink legislation and nearly take down a president. The mainstream press took notice.

According to December 2015 estimates by *Talkers Magazine*, Limbaugh had a cumulative weekly audience of around 13.25 million unique listeners (people listening for at least five minutes.) That volume of listeners made the Rush Limbaugh Show the most listened-to talk-radio program in the U.S. In the 1990s, Limbaugh's books "The Way Things Ought to Be" (1992) and "See, I Told You So" (1993) made The *New York Times* Best Seller list.

Limbaugh frequently criticizes, in his books and on his show, what he regards as liberal policies and politicians, as well as what he perceives as a pervasive liberal bias in major U.S. media. Limbaugh is among the highest paid people in U.S. media, signing a contract in 2008 for $400 million through 2016. In 2015, *Forbes magazine* listed his earnings at $79 million for the previous 12 months and ranked him the 11th highest earning celebrity in the world. His most recent contract, signed on July 31, 2016, will take his radio program to 2020, its 32nd year.

For the past 25 years, conservative talk radio has been a growth industry that has launched well-known personalities other than Limbaugh. Glenn Beck, Sean Hannity, and Mark Levin are among the more well-known members of a stable that goes scores deep both nationally and regionally in U.S. radio. On cable television, Bill O'Reilly hosted a nightly commentary show on Fox News for more than 20 years, and for 16 of those years, his was the highest-rated show on cable news.

The fact that conservative talk radio continues to be a growth industry spoke to Donald Trump in language he could understand, in more than one sense. Conservative talk radio is a growth industry because an ever-growing number of people are listening. Those listeners provide excellent ratings, which are monetized by advertising. The higher the ratings, the more advertisers are anxious to reach the audience, and rates therefore increase due to supply and demand.

Trump and his advisors listened to thousands of hours of conservative talk radio in the weeks and months leading up to the candidate's pronouncement in 2015 that he would build a great wall along the Mexican border. Trump and his staff knew what issues were important to this large sector of the electorate which felt overlooked by both parties.

These issues and Trump's positions on them produced a great opportunity for the candidate to talk to the hosts of these shows in language that everyone listening understood. Conservative talk radio listeners believed that perhaps finally there was a candidate who not only understood them but would listen to them and make their concerns a top priority if elected.

Many of them also felt that shows like Limbaugh's and Hannity's provided news that was more accurate than the "mainstream media." The public's opinion of the established news outlets was falling faster than their opinion of members of Congress and used car salespeople.

News is not free

In late 2016, the Gallup polling organization reported that Americans' trust and confidence in the mass media "to report the news fully, accurately and fairly" had dropped to its lowest level in the polling organization's history.

Only 32 percent of those surveyed said they have a great deal or fair amount of trust in the media — down eight percentage points from 2015.

Gallup began asking this question in 1972, and on a yearly basis since 1997. Over the history of the trend, Americans' trust and confidence hit its highest point in 1976, at 72 percent, in the wake of widely lauded examples of investigative journalism, including the Watergate scandal.[10] After staying in the low to mid-50s through the late 1990s and into the early years of the new century, Americans' trust in the media has fallen slowly and steadily. It has consistently been below a majority level since 2007.

The election campaign may be the reason the trust level fell so sharply in 2016, according to Gallup. With many Republican leaders and conservative pundits saying Hillary Clinton received overly positive media attention, while Donald Trump received unfair or negative attention, this may be the prime reason their relatively low trust in the media has evaporated even more, Gallup said.

"It is also possible that Republicans think less of the media as a result of Trump's sharp criticisms of the press. Republicans who say they have trust in the media has plummeted to 14 percent from 32 percent a year ago. This is easily the lowest confidence among Republicans in 20 years," a Gallup news release said.

A leaked email showed that Democratic National Committee boss and former CNN contributor Donna Brazile shared a debate question in advance with the Hillary Clinton campaign[11] — despite Brazile's persistent claims to the contrary. Brazile was on leave from her position with the Democratic National Committee and working with CNN when this occurred. While it is very unlikely that CNN news leaders knew Brazile would share information with her party's candidate, it certainly calls into question their judgment to allow Brazile access to debate subject matter.

A sports analogy would be the Dogs' quarterback is out for the year with an injury, so he takes a temporary position with a TV network as a game analyst. Before a contest between the Dogs and the Cats, the Cats' coach shares intimate details of his team's game plan with the TV announcers, who the coach presumes are unbiased because they are working for the media.

The sports director at the network would at least have to consider the possibility that the Dogs' quarterback would share the Cats' confidential game plan details with his team since he is merely on leave from them. The best decision for the sports director would be not to assign the Dogs' quarterback to cover the Cats because of the potential conflict of interest, and that's what CNN should have done in Brazile's case. It's that sort of terrible judgment that fuels the public mistrust of the mainstream media.

In 2015, Politico.com revealed that ABC News chief anchor George Stephanopoulos gave $75,000 to the Clinton Foundation[12], charitable contributions that he did not publicly disclose while reporting on the Clintons or their nonprofit organization.

In 2012, 2013 and 2014, Stephanopoulos made $25,000 donations to the 501 nonprofit founded by former President Bill Clinton, the foundation's records show. Stephanopoulos never disclosed this information to viewers, even when interviewing author Peter Schweizer about his book "Clinton Cash," which alleges that donations to the foundation may have influenced some of Hillary Clinton's actions as secretary of state.

Before joining ABC News, Stephanopoulos served as communications director and senior adviser for policy and strategy to President Clinton. He also served as communications director for Bill Clinton's 1992 presidential campaign.

Stephanopoulos has carved out a very prominent media career for himself in his life after Democratic Party politics. Even without the Clinton Foundation revelations, any observer of politics for the past few decades would know that he has close ties to the Clinton family. That, of course, would make any news consumer wonder if he would ask Hillary or Bill the tough questions. The revelation of the Clinton Foundation donations erased whatever shred of doubt existed.

It is the general practice in the news business for editors not to assign a story to a reporter who has a potential conflict of interest. This is to assure reporting of the most impartial and fair information. Stephanopoulos should have a) told his superiors at ABC News about his donations and b) recused himself from coverage of the Clintons.

But, that could be a career-killer for a national news anchor, to say that he can't cover the election campaign because of possible bias. ABC News said it was standing by its star anchor, saying he admitted to them "an honest mistake." If the truth meter were turned on, it probably would have translated the ABC News statement to, "We have a highly rated news anchor who would have to commit a much more egregious transgression than this for us to replace him. His high ratings on both Good Morning America and the evening news would be very difficult and costly for us to replace."

This type of bad judgment is not confined to one network or one side of the political spectrum. Fox News reporter and anchor Bret Baier, who hosts "Special Report" on the cable channel, apologized in November 2016 for reporting that indictments were "likely" in an ongoing investigation into the Clinton Foundation[13], adding that the reports were a mistake.

"All the time, but especially in a heated election on a topic this explosive, every word matters — no matter how well-sourced," Baier told Fox News' Jon Scott on a subsequent broadcast of "Happening Now." "Which brings me to this: I explained a couple of times yesterday the phrasing of one of my answers to (Fox News host) Brit Hume on Wednesday night, saying it was inartful the way I answered (a) question about whether the investigations would continue after the election. And I answered that, yes, our sources said it would, they would continue to likely an indictment. Well, that wasn't just inartful. It was a mistake. And for that, I'm sorry."

Baier apologized for the use of the word "indictment," but said he and the network stood by their reporting, despite not naming any of the sources who provided the information. As of the publication date of this book, there were no indictments relating to the Clinton Foundation investigation.

One of the primary reasons a report like that even makes it to a television news script is the now-common practice of using unnamed sources of tips and information. This has become common in all types of media, contrary to news policies of decades ago when this was not permitted. It was not allowed because the thought at the time was if the source was not willing to have the information attributed to him or her directly, how true or good could it be?

It was a way to ensure that news consumers received thoroughly vetted information. If a source lied to a reporter, the reader would know the identity of the liar because the information would be attributed. There would be a trail to follow if the information reported to the public proved to be incorrect or false. When unnamed sources are used, the only people who know the source of information are the reporter and his or her editor.

Not using a source's name makes that person much more likely to talk about something controversial or classified than someone who can be held accountable for making the statements. An easy way to track the prevalence of this practice is to visit http://schaver.com/anonymous for that website's Anonymous Source Tracker.

The website says it tracks these online news sources: ABC News, AL.com, Associated Press, BBC, Bleacher Report, Bloomberg, Boston Globe, Boston.com, Business Insider, BuzzFeed, CBS News, CNET, CNN, Chicago Tribune, Daily Beast, Daily Mail, Detroit Free Press, ESPN, Elite Daily, Engadget, Examiner, Fox News, Gawker, Guardian, Houston Chronicle, Huffington Post, Los Angeles Times, MIC,

MLive.com, MSN, Mashable, Mirror, NBC News, NJ.com, NPR, New York Daily News, New York Post, New York Times, Politico, Reuters, SFGate, Salon, Slate, Tech Crunch, Telegraph, The Atlantic, The Blaze, The Intercept, Time, U.S. News, USA Today, Upworthy, Vice, Vox, Wall Street Journal, Washington Post and Yahoo.

A February 2017 check of that website showed it displaying nearly 16,000 stories from these online news outlets that used anonymous sourcing. Those 16,000 stories covered about the previous 10 months. Do the math, and you learn that more than 1,500 stories produced monthly by the nation's larger news organizations contain anonymous sourcing.

Anonymous sources have a checkered journalistic history. None is more famous and perhaps more important than Watergate's "Deep Throat," the FBI source who helped Washington Post reporters Woodward and Bernstein unravel the White House involvement in and cover-up of the Watergate break-in.

"Deep Throat" was identified 31 years later as Mark Felt, the number two man in the FBI in the early 1970s. In the aftermath of the revelation of Felt's identity on May 31, 2005, a *Washington Post* story portrayed him as a man loyal to the mission of the FBI, but also concerned about what he saw as threats to the U.S. Constitution from the Nixon administration's activities.

During the peak of Woodward and Bernstein's reporting, Nixon reportedly was furious that the FBI was "leaking like a sieve." This history may explain President Trump's worries early in 2017:

> **Donald J. Trump** ✓ @realDonaldTrump · Feb 16
> ## The spotlight has finally been put on the low-life leakers! They will be caught!
>
> ⤺   ↻ 26K   ♥ 127K

A very important distinction to remember about "Deep Throat:" The *Washington Post* used him as an indirect source. Because he was unwilling to have his name or anything about his background revealed, journalism ethics of the time required Woodward and Bernstein to track down and independently verify his claims through sources other than him. If the reporters had gone to *Post* Editor Ben Bradlee with a story of the magnitude of Watergate, based on quotes and information from an unnamed source, they would have been laughed out of his office and possibly fired.

The *Post*'s Watergate reporting was based on independent verification of every claim an anonymous source made, not by attributing any of the Post's claims directly to the anonymous source.

But these days, as an indirect effect of Watergate, anonymity is the name of the Washington game. Everyone seems to be an administration or congressional source or a law enforcement or military source. These "sources" get information and stories about potential legislation into the media without direct attribution, often to gauge public reaction before a plan or proposal beforehand.

Reporters must let their bosses know who their unnamed sources are, so at least the management of the media company knows on whose word they are taking the risk of being wrong. In most cases, unnamed sources are people whose names you might recognize, but because media standards have become so lax, there is no need for them to agree to have their names used. The result is an environment in which people with an ax to grind can do so without having to deal directly with any of the fallout.

The Society of Professional Journalists Code of Ethics contains two pointed statements on anonymous sources[14]:

1. Identify sources whenever feasible. The public is entitled to as much information as possible on sources' reliability.

The most important professional possession of journalists is credibility. If the news consumers don't have faith that the stories they are reading or watching are accurate and fair, if they suspect information attributed to an anonymous source has been made up, then the journalists are as useful as a parka at the equator.

2. Always question sources' motives before promising anonymity. Clarify conditions attached to any promise made in exchange for information. Keep promises.

The information-gathering business is a give-and-take practice with a lot of public officials. Some are willing to provide information only when it benefits them. When someone asks to provide information off the record, be sure the reason is not to boost her own position by undermining someone else's, to even the score with a rival, to attack an opponent or to push a personal agenda.

So why do media outlets permit this? It's because the competition for news consumption is as fierce as it ever has been.

In the 1950s and 1960s, you got national news from three TV networks at specific times of the day. You had your newspaper delivered at the appointed time, and you also had local TV and radio stations that delivered local news. Throw in magazines, and you had probably no more than a dozen different sources for the typical news consumer.

Today, in the era of the Internet and social media, the typical news and information consumer has access to many hundreds of more sources of news, many catering to specific interests such as entertainment, sports and politics. Every person with a smartphone can become a reporter.

If you take away nothing else from this book, remember that news is not free. It may seem that news is free because we rarely pay for it anymore. But every news organization has overhead, salaries and benefits to pay. The revenue to pay for most those expenses comes from paid advertising. The larger audience you have, the more that advertisers will want to use your medium to reach possible customers. On the other hand, if your audience declines, so does the demand by advertisers to buy an ad on your page or during your show.

As the number of news outlets has exploded in recent years, so has the fragmentation of retail dollars spent on media. The businesses in your town in the 1960s knew that there were about 12 good ways to reach you with an offer. The businesses in your town today know that there are hundreds of ways to reach you, and frankly, they are confused as to the best way to do it. Instead of a dozen media sales representatives soliciting them for advertising, these days there are dozens. These changes have meant tremendous upheaval in the business side of news organizations, which no longer can count on the legacy advertising dollars flowing in that used to be all but a sure thing less than a half-century ago.

The media as we used to know it has been as affected by the changes in the ways we consume media in the past 50 years in ways the average news consumer doesn't understand.

Between 2013 and 2015 alone, the 25 largest daily newspapers in the U.S. lost an astounding 35 percent of their combined paid circulation. The biggest loser was *USA Today*, which went from 1.424 million daily paid circulation in 2013 to only 299,000 two years later.[15] This isolated two-year period reflects a trend that is nearly a century in the making.

Remember the 1960s, when there were about a dozen media sources to which you had daily access? Turn the clock even further back to 1910, when there was not yet any radio or TV. Companies that owned newspaper printing presses, in effect, were printing money. Anyone who needed to advertise knew the way to do it was to put an ad in the paper. For a news consumer, there was only one place to turn, and that was the local newspaper.

The national trend in declining circulation began as first radio, and then television became more widely available and provided news content that didn't require payment. But most consumers still realized that the newspaper companies had the most reporters and the resources to do the most thorough reporting. The circulation decline, while evident, was not a game-changer for the industry ... yet.

In the 1970s and 1980s, as more and more households had both spouses working, there was less time in each household's daily schedule to sit and read the news. Around this time, most larger cities still had a morning paper and an afternoon paper, but the afternoon paper was quickly going the way of the dinosaur. If there was a time of day to read the paper, it was in the morning before the work day got started. By the time both spouses got home from work, they were scurrying to get dinner fixed and to take the kids to their extra-curricular activities. If there was time after work for news, it was to be listened to or watched while some other household-centric activity was taking place.

The biggest cultural shift to affect the newspaper industry, of course, has been the ability of the everyday consumer to read news online. As personal computers became more and more prevalent in the 1990s, people turned to written news content for which they didn't have to pay.

In what historians may look back on as the ultimate death knell of the newspaper industry, many of the large newspapers – concerned that they were losing market share in a big way – began posting the content that was in their paid printed publications on free websites. The rationale was that the newspaper companies did not want to lose their share in their markets, and would cater to the growing number of people who were going online for news by giving it to them there. At that time, there was no online subscription model that worked, so the newspaper companies tried to generate revenue online by posting paid banner ads on their news pages.

What they learned is that advertisers were not willing to pay the same rate to advertise online as they were to advertise in print. That remains an issue today for all media companies.

Companies buy advertising for two primary reasons: to spur direct sales, or for branding, the process of building familiarity with a company name or product name.

A direct sales ad wants to motivate you to do something today, right now, as you look at the ad. The advertiser wants you to do something like click on the ad, call a number, immediately get to the store – all so you can buy, sign up for or download something today.

The advertiser tallies the direct responses to the ad and measures the effectiveness of the ad.

Branding advertisers learned banner ads are not the most effective vehicle for branding. Compared to a magazine ad or a TV ad, banner ads are small and easily ignored. Direct sales advertisers learned that the response rate for banner ads is low. For most banner ads, the industry average seems to hover between two and five clicks per 1,000 impressions (sets of eyeballs seeing the ad).[16] What that means is, if a banner ad appears 1,000 times on web pages, between two and five people who see the ad will click it to learn more.

Those five clicks per 1,000 impressions don't have much value to most advertisers. The reason is that those five clicks will not all generate sales. Out of 100 clicks, perhaps one person will do the desired thing (buy something, download something, etc.).

Here's an example. Let's say that a publisher wants people to buy a book, and hopes to increase sales of the book through advertising. The publisher has budgeted $3 per copy of the book to spend on advertising. If the publisher is paying $30 per 1,000 impressions for banner ads and purchases 100,000 impressions for $3,000, here is what happens:

- The banner ad appears 100,000 times.
- Let's say the response rate is five clicks per 1,000 impressions, so 500 people click on the ad during the time the 100,000 total impressions are running.
- If 2 percent of those 500 people purchase the book, that results in 10 purchases.
- The publisher had to pay $300 ($3,000 divided by 10) for each book purchased through that ad.

Obviously, paying $300 to sell one book is not a good economic model for a publisher, especially since the budget is $3 per book. For this type of advertising to work for the publisher, he would need to pay 30 cents per 1,000 impressions, rather than 30 dollars.

So banner ad rates began to decline. Today, if you shop around, you can buy banner ads from thousands of Web sites or brokers for 50 cents or so per thousand impressions — which is pretty much exactly what they are worth to a person who is trying to sell something with banner ads using a direct sales model.

It is possible for some websites to charge more than 50 cents per 1,000 impressions. For example, the top 100 or so websites can charge a premium because of their size. There is also a process called targeting. For example, if you want to sell a laptop computer, you can advertise on a website that provides information for people interested in buying a laptop. That's a targeted audience for your ad, which will typically increase the click-through and response rate for the ad. Yahoo and many search engines target their banner ads to the search words people type in, and they charge more for these targeted ads. But for most other Web sites, there is very little money to be made from banner ads.

Here is the dilemma newspapers and the other "legacy media" (television and radio) face: Let's be generous and say that a legacy media website has a million page views per day. (The largest ones might, but 99 percent do not.) An advertiser who pays 50 cents per 1,000 impressions on the website would pay $500 for 1 million impressions in that day.

Compare that to what a newspaper would charge for a print "display" ad – an ad that does not appear in the classified section, but on the same page as news content. Printed publications charge for advertising by the column inch, which is about a two-inch by one-inch block of space. Per column inch, the larger newspapers still charge around $1,000. So, for a 20-inch ad, the fee would be somewhere around $20,000 for that day's ad.

One of the major problems for the newspaper industry is that more and more people are buying advertising at that $500 rate (for online ads) than at the $20,000 rate (for print ads), because more and more of the people they want to reach are consuming content online instead of in print. TV and radio companies charge for advertising by the minute, or fractions thereof, and are in precisely the same boat.

There are always going to be forms of advertising better suited to legacy media than online banner ads. But the migration of eyeballs is unmistakable, and advertisers are following suit.

The only companies that have truly mastered the online revenue equation are Facebook, Google, and Amazon – and none of their businesses are remotely similar in modality to a newspaper.

One that is, though, is Craigslist. When Craigslist started offering free online classified advertising in the late 1990s, it had the effect of a dagger to the heart of one of the newspaper industry's top revenue sources. (Craigslist uses free classifieds to get customers "in the door." Once they are satisfied customers, they are willing to pay for some types of ads, such as Help Wanted.)

Remember when that big Sunday paper delivered to your house had a huge section of classified ads? Every inch on each of those pages was paid for – unquestionably the biggest profit center of the industry.

You may be saying, "Wait, I pay for my paper every day. Isn't every inch of every page paid for? By me and everyone else who buys it?" The truth is, the price you pay to have the paper delivered covers only the cost the newspaper company pays the delivery person to bring it to you. When you put coins in a newspaper vending box, you just reimbursed the newspaper company the cost it paid to the person who brought the papers to the box and loaded it. You didn't cover any of the costs associated with creating that newspaper.

If newspaper companies charged the reader the actual cost to create a newspaper, it would be at least $20 per page. This is to pay the reporters, the editors, the people who run the press and the internal business staff, along with overhead including tons and tons of paper rolls known as newsprint. So, a 100-page Sunday paper would run you a cool $2,000. All the paid ads in the paper make it possible for the newspaper company to charge much less than that.

Newspapers publishing online nowadays are doing so for a small fraction of the revenue they earn from print advertising. While the revenue for these companies has been consistently diminishing for decades, so has the staffing level. There are fewer and fewer reporters and editors because the revenue no longer supports staff sizes as they once were.

We often see these days examples of major mistakes made in headlines and other aspects of newspapers, and the kneejerk reaction is to say, "Well, that's why that industry is dying." In fact, you have maybe one-third to one-quarter of the reporters and editors who worked to put out a daily newspaper 20 to 30 years ago now trying to do the same job. Newspaper people are among the most dedicated professionals you'll find, but they have been through the career wringer for the past few decades. As new young talent comes in, the veterans who used to stay for a full career and help to mentor newcomers are long gone.

There may be no better example of just where the newspaper industry is financially than the November 2016 announcement that The *Detroit News* offered a buyout to *all* its newsroom employees in an attempt to meet its 2017 budget requirement.[17]

A month later, the newspaper announced its sports editor, assistant managing editor, assistant photo editor and a sports copy editor would be leaving, and that more cuts were still needed.[18]

Buyout offers have been common in recent years in the newspaper business, but they usually are made with the idea of keeping certain key personnel in place. The *Detroit News* told its staff and the world that they didn't care who put their hand up, just so the final total met corporate budget needs. In effect, it didn't matter if all the senior reporters and editors took the offer and left an inexperienced staff with no veteran leaders or mentors. (At the time this book was written, there was no final tally on how many and who accepted the offer.)

Back to the question of why do media companies allow the use of anonymous sources: With literally an innumerable number of news outlets available to any person at any one time, the primary way to gain the attention of news consumers is to be first with a story. These days, if you are not first, you are last. Being first means people are more likely to respond to alerts about breaking news on their mobile devices. And those folks are more likely to share it via their social media networks, increasing the chance of a story going "viral."

If two news outlets have the same story, and one decides to go with it using an unnamed source, while the other holds it for further vetting and getting an on-the-record confirmation, the unnamed-source story is going to make it online first. And while it certainly is not the most complete or most vetted story, it achieves the business goal of being first – greatly increasing the number of shares and click-throughs (and as an extension, impressions) over subsequent versions.

Click-throughs are the key to revenue in today's digital media economy. Most high-volume websites include advertising that pays the website owner based on how many impressions the web page gets. Clicks on the ads themselves are another revenue stream.

Electronic news sources like radio and television are not immune from the need to post information online as soon as possible. They are now on a level playing field with the newspapers in many ways, because they are subject to the same low market rates for banner advertising as newspapers or anyone else who owns a website.

And lest you think that radio and television are immune from the same competitive issues as newspapers have fallen victim to, think again. Those two media are scrambling to devise strategies to avoid what has befallen the newspaper industry.

Local news is the leading revenue generator for local television stations. All the ads during the 30- to 60-minute local news programs are local ads, sold by the station, which gets 100 percent of the revenue. On the other hand, programs that originate from networks or syndication contain mostly ads that were sold by the program originators. The local stations, therefore, receive very little, if any, of that revenue.

Television stations have marketed to you for years to be sure to watch the news in the early morning, at 5 and 6 p.m. and the late news, because they want as many eyeballs on their programs (and accompanying ads) as possible.

But have you noticed how many websites now feature video? In keeping with the be-first-not-last concept, many news companies now put their news video online as quickly as possible. What this means is that you no longer have to wait until 5, 6, 10, or 11 to see local news video. That means there is less need to make sure you are watching the TV at 5, 6, 10 and 11 to catch the important news, and therefore, you are less likely to view the ads that accompany the local news. It is now "on-demand," toward which every other form of media consumption is rapidly evolving.

Television stations are now facing the same crunch newspapers did – the pressure to compete in the new online marketplace. Text was the original primary medium of online communication, and now video is quickly catching up.

On Election Night 2016, all the major networks were streaming their election coverage on Facebook Live. If television screens alone were enough to reach a significant portion of the audience, they would have been content to be there alone. But those Facebook Live video streams were an indication that the networks all know they will need a significant online presence for mobile devices moving forward. Facebook, as usual, was ahead of the curve – being first to market with an easy-to-use platform for instant live video.

Radio? Its primary mission is delivering entertainment, not news. But websites like Pandora and Spotify now allow anyone to set up personal channels with customized music selections. No longer do you have to listen to the pop station and hope you hear a Michael Jackson song occasionally. Now you can set up your personal channel to be as narrowly focused as you want, 24-7. Broadcast radio can't compete with this.

How often have you heard someone say, "All I want is a news organization that reports just the facts and nothing but the facts?" Because of the factors outlined in this chapter, that model is no longer economically feasible. If every news organization did that, they would all be the same. In today's media economy, you must stand out to be noticed and get eyeballs on your ads to generate the revenue to cover the costs of doing business (and hopefully generate a profit). Be first or be last.

Fox News and MSNBC understood this trend many years ago. They quickly realized that becoming merely a copy of CNN — their primary competitor in the 24-hour news channel niche — would be a path to financial red ink. So, they catered to specific political mindsets – MSNBC went Democratic / liberal, and Fox News went Republican / conservative.

Those were brilliant business strategies. Data from Nielsen, the company that gathers viewership data that helps determine ratings, showed that Fox News was the most-watched of the cable news channels for the 15th straight year in 2016. MSNBC's ratings showed substantial year-over-year improvement in 2016 compared to 2015, though the network still finished third behind Fox and CNN.

As mentioned earlier, conservative-based media is a growth market and continues to grow in the wake of the 2016 election. Fox News's dominance in cable news is attributable to that business decision made many years ago, recognizing an underserved market.

A "just-the-facts" approach to news delivery traditionally did not incorporate political favoritism. But the company that is standing out among cable news providers went that route. Fox's high ratings have brought great financial success, much like the conservative radio talk shows. And make no mistake, other news providers are looking for a way to gain attention and consumer eyeballs just like Fox.

Have you ever heard someone say, "Why can't there be more good news stories on the news?" The simple reason is that good news doesn't sell. An old saying in the news media business is, "If it bleeds, it leads." News consumers have historically shown that they react to the sensational. A newspaper company will sell many more copies on a day which pictures of a major fire or building collapse display in the windows of the newspaper vending boxes, rather than a picture of a cute puppy or outstanding student.

It's probably not a surprise, but the sensational also sells online. The website Allora.io[19] claims to have cataloged more than 150,000 websites using a product called Taboola. At the bottom of online news articles, you will often see links like "This game will keep you up all night," or "Ivanka Trump says this is the one thing you should do before firing someone." They are "teasers," also known as "click-bait," provided to thousands of websites by Taboola:

You May Also Like
Sponsored Links by Taboola

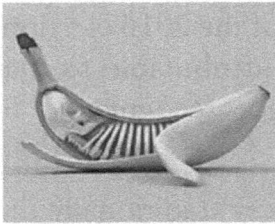

The Root Of All Stomach Problems - Avoid These 3 Foods
BIOX4 Supplement

25+ Perfectly Timed Photos That Almost Broke The Internet
Auto Overload

Actress Ma... ocks Us With He... Solution T...
ActivatedYou Supplement

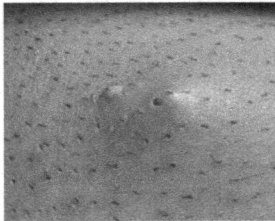

This Simple Skin Fix May Surprise You
Primal Plants Supplement · Gundry

10 Deleted Scenes That Changed The Movie
Detonate

25 Surprising Things The US President Cannot Do
Frank151

Companies with provocative content pay Taboola a fee to make a link to their content available to the tens of thousands of websites that display Taboola content. Taboola pays the websites which display what it refers to as its "recommendations" for each click. That revenue is the external websites' motivation. Taboola claims to serve over 200 billion "recommendations" (impressions) to over 550 million unique visitors each month.[20]

The fact that sensational and salacious content is money-making for both its originators and the companies that publish links to it should come as no real surprise. The *National Enquirer* continues to publish nearly 100 years after its founding, an indication that no matter how often you hear people pooh-pooh it, there is an audience that is buying it and will continue to buy it. Sensationalism sells.

Many people believe that the quality and accuracy of news coverage has diminished because of specific political biases on the part of media. But legacy media struggling to compete at the much-lower online revenue rates, and the directly related diminishing newsroom staff sizes, are at least as important. When you have one person doing the job that three or four people did just a few decades ago (as is the case in most newsrooms), there is no question that the product will suffer.

When you have a technology that has changed the world in about 20 years like personal computers, and now smartphones, have, people want their content on those devices. Media companies are desperate to figure out how to maintain the quality of their product while an ever-increasing portion of their revenue is coming from the comparatively low-revenue-producing banner ad.

Until they figure it out, they know they have to get to you first with the news, or be last. That's why you occasionally see reporting that is fraught with mistakes or gaping holes. In many cases, you are consuming news from companies now staffing skeleton crews, compared to how many people they employed at the peak of their financial success.

These are among the reasons why non-mainstream digital news outlets like The Drudge Report and The Huffington Post have gained tremendous market share. They knew what the banner ads would pay, and they built a business structure around it – unlike the "traditional" media, which built its business structures around revenue streams dozens of times higher at the time of their inception.

Drudge and HuffPost are two more examples of news media that consciously sought out readers in specific political niches, conservative and liberal, respectively.

In June 2015, the HuffPost made the following announcement on its website:

> After watching and listening to Donald Trump since he announced his candidacy for president, we have decided we won't report on Trump's campaign as part of The Huffington Post's political coverage. Instead, we will cover his campaign as part of our Entertainment section. Our reason is simple: Trump's campaign is a sideshow. We won't take the bait. If you are interested in what The Donald has to say, you'll find it next to our stories on the Kardashians and The Bachelorette.

With that statement, the HuffPost disqualified itself as an impartial news source. If you wanted to know what was happening in the campaign of one of the leading presidential candidates in the Republican party, there was no point visiting the HuffPost's news pages. As we have outlined in this chapter, news producers and publishers have a higher priority than impartiality, and that is economic survival. The HuffPost did not experience any significant backlash from its decision among its primarily liberal-leaning readership. That's because it's human nature for people to favor information which reinforces their pre-existing views, while at the same time avoiding contradictory information.

Psychologists call the theory "selective exposure:" Upon exposure to specific aspects of information, people tend to incorporate specific portions into their mindset. These choices are made based on their perspectives, beliefs, attitudes and decisions. People mentally dissect the information to which they are exposed, and tend to select favorable evidence while ignoring the unfavorable.

In the early 1960s, Columbia University researcher Joseph T. Klapper asserted in his book "The Effects Of Mass Communication" that audiences were not passive targets of political and commercial propaganda from mass media, but that mass media reinforces their previously held convictions.

Throughout the book, he argued that the media has a small amount of power to influence people and, most of the time, it just reinforces our preexisting attitudes and beliefs. He argued that the media effects of relaying or spreading new public messages or ideas were minimal because there is a wide variety of ways in which individuals filter such content. Due to this tendency, Klapper argued that media content must be able to ignite some type of cognitive activity in an individual in order to communicate its message.

An example of this is the rush to be first with a story. As a reader, you are more likely to react to something the first time you read or hear about it, particularly if it is unfamiliar or sensational. After your first consumption of a story, you are much less likely to click on the same story from other news outlets. The newness of a story ignites the cognitive activities of surprise and curiosity.

Before Klapper's research, the prevailing opinion was that mass media had a substantial power to sway individual opinion and that audiences were passive consumers of prevailing media propaganda. However, Klapper's research showed that people gravitated towards media messages that bolstered previously held convictions set by their peer groups, societal influences, and family structures. This did not change over time, even when presented with more recent media messages.

Klapper noted that audiences were selective to the types of programming that they consumed. Adults would patronize media that was appropriate for their demographics and children would steer clear of media that was boring to them. Individuals would either accept or reject a mass media message based upon internal filters that were innate to that person.

This also helps to explain the extreme level of bitterness and distaste we often see people on one side of the political divide have for people from the other side. The messages from the niche media are not only supportive of the people and positions from the side you are on, but hyper-critical of the other side. If your selective exposure has you inclined to believe that all ideas on your side of the spectrum are great, you may also believe that ideas from the other side are garbage and perhaps even dangerous.

To take that a step further, you may believe thanks to selective exposure that someone who supports the latter beliefs, by association, has a garbage personality and perhaps is even dangerous — even though there is a 99.9999 percent chance that is not the case at all.

Some researchers suggest that because consumers now hold more influence over the information provided to them by the media, consumers tend to select content that exposes and confirms their own ideas while avoiding information that argues against their opinion. Politics are more likely to inspire selective exposure among consumers than single-exposure decisions.

In one study, different types of media were compared and evaluated to see which type ignited the most selective exposure.[21] Due to the modern media atmosphere, people are now able to engage with or avoid the information that is presented to them to its fullest extent. Four different types of media were investigated in this study: newspapers, political talk radio, cable news, and political websites. Results showed that newspapers had less of an influence compared to cable news. Evidence clearly shows that people's political predispositions motivate their types of media selections.

A 2012 study by Solomon Messing and Sean J. Westwood of Stanford University showed that endorsements of an article by a friend on social media also had great influence.[22] This is a form of selective exposure: endorsement from a friend makes a person more likely to look at an article than other similar articles on social media that are not endorsed by friends.

Related to selective exposure is selective perception, a form of bias that causes people to perceive messages and actions according to their frame of reference. Using selective perception, people tend to overlook or forget information that contradicts their beliefs or expectations.

The key points in this chapter:

- Historically low public confidence in the "mainstream" media
- Lower standards for news organizations
- Legacy news media fighting for its financial existence
- Ever-increasing consumer reliance on online sources of news
- Success of niche news media
- The human tendency to select favorable information, while ignoring the unfavorable

all paved the way for the explosion of "fake news" that was one of the leading story lines, and perhaps even deciding factors, of the 2016 presidential election.

A perfect storm for fake news

Organizations that employ trained journalists to produce news content have one thing in common with the people behind the outbreak of "fake news:" they are both motivated by profit.

BuzzFeed.com reported in November 2016 that the town of Veles in the former Yugoslavian Republic of Macedonia became one of the global focal points for the generation of fake news.[23]

A group of digital entrepreneurs in this town of about 45,000 people launched at least 140 websites focusing on U.S. politics. The domain names were American-sounding:

- USConservativeToday.com

- WorldPoliticus.com

- TrumpVision365.com

- DonaldTrumpNews.co

- USADailyPolitics.com

- and many others.

They almost all publish aggressively pro-Trump content aimed at conservatives and Trump supporters in the United States.

The young Macedonians who ran these sites told BuzzFeed.com they don't care about Donald Trump; rather, they were responding to simple economic incentives: According to Facebook earnings reports, a U.S. Facebook user is worth about four times a user outside the U.S. The fraction-of-a-penny-per-click of U.S. display advertising goes a long way in Veles.

Several teens and young men who run these sites told BuzzFeed News that they learned the best way to generate traffic was to get their politics stories to spread on Facebook — and the best way to generate shares on Facebook was to publish sensationalist and often false content that caters to Trump supporters.

As a result, this strange hub of pro-Trump sites played a significant role in propagating false and misleading content. But at least in this particular case, the motivation was not political, but rather monetary. These sites open a window to the economic incentives behind producing misinformation targeted at the wealthiest advertising markets — and specifically for Facebook, the world's largest social network, as well as within online advertising networks such as Google AdSense.

Most of the posts on these sites are curated, or completely plagiarized, from fringe and right-wing sites in the United States. The Macedonians saw a story elsewhere, wrote a sensationalized headline, and quickly posted it to their site. Then they shared it on Facebook to try and generate traffic. The more people who clicked through from Facebook, the more money they earned from ads on their website.

Earlier in 2016, some in Veles experimented with left-leaning or pro–Bernie Sanders content, but nothing performed as well on Facebook as Trump content, BuzzFeed reported.

The flood of "fake news" in the 2016 election season received support from a sophisticated Russian propaganda campaign that created and spread misleading articles online with the goal of punishing Democrat Hillary Clinton, helping Republican Donald Trump and undermining faith in American democracy, according to a *Washington Post* report:[24]

"Russia's increasingly sophisticated propaganda machinery — including thousands of botnets, teams of paid human "trolls," and networks of websites and social-media accounts — echoed and amplified right-wing sites across the Internet as they portrayed Clinton as a criminal hiding potentially fatal health problems and preparing to hand control of the nation to a shadowy cabal of global financiers. The effort also sought to heighten the appearance of international tensions and promote fear of looming hostilities with nuclear-armed Russia."

The *Post* said researchers portrayed it as part of a broadly effective strategy of sowing distrust in U.S. democracy and its leaders. The tactics included penetrating the computers of election officials in several states and releasing troves of hacked emails that embarrassed Clinton in the final months of her campaign.

"They want to essentially erode faith in the U.S. government or U.S. government interests," Clint Watts, a fellow at the Foreign Policy Research Institute who along with two other researchers has tracked Russian propaganda since 2014, told the *Post*. "This was their standard mode during the Cold War. The problem is that this was hard to do before social media."

While Russia's political motivations are easy to understand, those of the Macedonians are a little less so. If a click only nets a payment of a fraction of a penny, is that worth the time and effort?

MarketWatch.com, along with several other mainstream news sources, in November 2016 profiled Paul Horner, who claimed that he makes $10,000 per month from advertising revenue streams tied to the fake news stories he posts online.[25]

On December 12, 2016, Horner posted a story with the headline, "Obama Signs Executive Order Declaring Investigation Into Election Results; Revote Planned For Dec. 19th."[26] The *Post* reported that the story had received more than 250,000 shares on Facebook. The website URL was abcnews.com.co – strikingly like ABC News's abcnews.com. The extreme similarity may have caused people to think after a quick glance that they were looking at an actual ABC News report. (By February 2017, Facebook had blocked people from sharing content from this URL "because it includes content that other people on Facebook have reported as abusive.")

During a February 2017 check of the "revote" story, the ABCNews.com.co website had the following "bio" of the "reporter" who wrote the story below the article:

Jimmy Rustling, ABC News

Born at an early age, Jimmy Rustling has found solace and comfort knowing that his humble actions have made this multiverse a better place for every man, woman and child ever known to exist. Dr. Jimmy Rustling has won many awards for excellence in writing including fourteen Peabody awards and a handful of Pulitzer Prizes. When Jimmies are not being Rustled the kind Dr. enjoys being an amazing husband to his beautiful, soulmate; Anastasia, a Russian mail order bride of almost 2 months. Dr. Rustling also spends 12-15 hours each day teaching their adopted 8-year-old Syrian refugee daughter how to read and write.

There is no attempt here to hide the fact that there is non-factual information on the page. When asked by the *Post* about how his "business" is different than it was a few years ago, Horner said, "Honestly, people are definitely dumber. They just keep passing stuff around. Nobody fact-checks anything anymore — I mean, that's how Trump got elected. He just said whatever he wanted, and people believed everything, and when the things he said turned out not to be true, people didn't care because they'd already accepted it. It's real scary. I've never seen anything like it."[27]

Horner's U.S.-based fake news sites generate revenue by displaying Google AdSense ads. Website owners can add blocks of code provided by Google to their websites, and ads served by Google will display in the spots on the site where the code is placed. Google is the middleman. Advertisers pay Google to distribute their ads to websites around the country and the world through this method.

Google says that publishers displaying Google AdSense ads on their websites receive 68 percent of the revenue. By being "first" with news, even fake news, publishers increase the "virality" and sharing of such content. If the story is salacious enough, it can generate tens of thousands or even hundreds of thousands of impressions.

Referring to our example in the last chapter, a million impressions cost about $500: If you ran a fake news website and could generate a million impressions on 20 different stories during a month, you would generate $10,000. Or, you could do the same with hundreds of stories generating far fewer impressions per story.

Google and Facebook are the engines which spark the virality of a news story. Both companies have established algorithms which rank stories by the number of clicks and views they receive. In both cases, a click or a view is considered a vote, in a sense. A story that receives a million clicks will be rated higher than a story that gets a half-million clicks. There are other factors in the algorithms, but interest by readers is the biggest factor.

Google News has a specific process by which websites can apply for inclusion in its news listings. Once accepted, news sites have their content "spidered" (reviewed) by Google several times an hour, to ensure that breaking news is detected and added to Google search results as soon as possible. This is different from non-news websites, which Google's "spiders" may visit once every day, week or month in search of new content to add to its search engine listings.

Google's spiders visit news sites more frequently because news can break at any time, not just once a day, week or month. This is how Google attempts to be first, not last, in the news game. And for the website that can get the top spot in a hot Google search about breaking news, the financial rewards can be amazing. News sources that are an hour or two behind miss the initial surge of searches from people who are just hearing about breaking news and wanting to know more. Therefore, they miss a huge number of potential clicks and page impressions. If you're not first, you're last.

Google has stated it will actively search out websites that publish fake news and turn off the revenue spigot to those sites. But the truth is that individuals or companies making $10,000 per month or more via revenue from fake news will just start up new sites at new domains under fake names when Google shuts them down. When your enforcement world consists of literally billions of websites, as does Google's, it can take a bit of time to find one that is trying to lay low.

Facebook's algorithms for determining which stories got top ratings on its site took on even greater prominence after August 2016, when the company fired its human-being news curators.

After the November 2016 election, many people blamed Facebook for spreading partisan — and largely pro-Trump — fake news, such as Pope Francis's alleged endorsement of Trump, or Hillary Clinton's supposedly secret life-threatening illness. The company was criticized for prioritizing user "engagement," meaning that its algorithms boosted juicy fake news over other kinds of stories. Those algorithms took on greater prominence after Facebook fired its small team of human beings who curated its "trending" news section in August 2016, following conservative complaints that it was biased against the right.

After the election, Facebook hired third-party fact checkers such as those behind the Snopes and Politifact websites to help detect fake news sources. They did so because they did not want to face again the charges of political bias by humans employed by Facebook playing a role in the social media giant's ranking of news stories.

In December 2016, Facebook published the following information in a post called "Addressing Hoaxes and Fake News" on its newsroom blog:[28]

> ... We believe in giving people a voice and that we cannot become arbiters of truth ourselves, so we're approaching this problem carefully. We've focused our efforts on the worst of the worst, on the clear hoaxes spread by spammers for their own gain, and on engaging both our community and third party organizations.
>
> The work falls into the following four areas. These are just some of the first steps we're taking to improve the experience for people on Facebook. We'll learn from these tests, and iterate and extend them over time.
>
> **Easier Reporting**
>
> We're testing several ways to make it easier to report a hoax if you see one on Facebook, which you can do by clicking the upper right hand corner of a post. We've relied heavily on our community for help on this issue, and this can help us detect more fake news.
>
> **Flagging Stories as Disputed**
>
> We believe providing more context can help people decide for themselves what to trust and what to share. We've started a program to

work with third-party fact checking organizations that are signatories of Poynter's International Fact Checking Code of Principles. We'll use the reports from our community, along with other signals, to send stories to these organizations. If the fact checking organizations identify a story as fake, it will get flagged as disputed and there will be a link to the corresponding article explaining why. Stories that have been disputed may also appear lower in News Feed.

It will still be possible to share these stories, but you will see a warning that the story has been disputed as you share.

Once a story is flagged, it can't be made into an ad and promoted, either.

Informed Sharing

We're always looking to improve News Feed by listening to what the community is telling us. We've found that if reading an article makes people significantly less likely to share it, that may be a sign that a story has misled people in some way. We're going to test incorporating this signal into ranking, specifically for articles that are outliers, where people who read the article are significantly less likely to share it.

Disrupting Financial Incentives for Spammers

We've found that a lot of fake news is financially motivated. Spammers make money by masquerading as well-known news organizations, and posting hoaxes that get people to visit to their sites, which are often mostly ads. So we're doing several things to reduce the financial incentives. On the buying side we've eliminated the ability to spoof domains, which will reduce the prevalence of sites that pretend to be real publications. On the publisher side, we are analyzing publisher sites to detect where policy enforcement actions might be necessary. ...

Most of the afore-mentioned fake news stories got the fuel for their virality from Facebook, which – as of February 2017 – had 1.86 billion active monthly users worldwide.

More than 40 percent of American adults get news via Facebook, according to a 2016 report published by the Pew Research Center and the Knight Foundation.

Two-thirds of Facebook users access news on the social platform, and with 67 percent of U.S. adults active on Facebook, that translates to 44 percent of the overall U.S. population which accesses news on the social platform, the study said.[29]

The numbers above provide perspective on how a hot news story – true or fake – can receive mind-boggling numbers of impressions (and revenue from impressions and clicks) in short order.

Like Google, Facebook does not produce news content. Both Internet giants aggregate content from outside sources, and present it in a hierarchy determined by computer algorithms.

The financial motivations for content distributors of both true and fake news are clear. What is also clear is that the growing number of news consumers who don't trust what they are reading or hearing have reason to be disillusioned and confused.

Any news consumer is best served by getting information from an organization that pays journalists to gather content which is then vetted by editors. The mainstream media companies are not paying these individuals millions and millions of dollars collectively as a ruse to fool news consumers into believing they are doing their best to report the truth. The mainstream news companies are paying their reporters and editors to report factual information.

Are mistakes made? Unfortunately, yes. Reporters and editors are people, too – people who in many cases are working in newsrooms with skeleton-crew staffing levels, compared to years ago. The rush to be first, not last, can also lead to errors in judgment or simple carelessness.

It's more important than ever for news consumers to question every bit of news information, particularly political. Is the reporting organization a legitimate news organization? Is the information attributed to unnamed sources? Does the information make any sense? For example, does it make any sense at all for the Pope to endorse Donald Trump?

For all the reasons outlined heretofore, even the most trusting news consumer now should question the authenticity of any report that has any political element.

The news consumers who don't want to ponder which report is true and which one is false have instead opted for the selective exposure that is part of their human nature. In effect, if the report agrees with their personal line of thinking, it must be true. And if it doesn't, it must be false ...

... which has helped to lead us to the era of post-truth politics in America.

Post-truth: emotions before facts

Oxford Dictionaries declared "post-truth" their word of the year for 2016. The term refers to a version of reporting and campaigning in which appealing to emotions is more important than factual accuracy.

The word has existed for more than two decades, but a rise in its demand coincided with the EU "Brexit" referendum and the U.S. presidential race, Oxford Dictionaries said.

Casper Grathwohl, president of Oxford Dictionaries, said: "It's not surprising that our choice reflects a year dominated by highly-charged political and social discourse. Fuelled by the rise of social media as a news source and a growing distrust of facts offered up by the establishment, 'post-truth' as a concept has been finding its linguistic footing for some time."

The dictionary defines "post-truth" as: "Relating to or denoting circumstances in which objective facts are less influential in shaping public opinion than appeals to emotion and personal belief." (Note the effect of selective exposure.)

Its earliest usage with this meaning was in a 1992 essay on the Iran-Contra scandal and the Gulf War by playwright Steve Tesich in The Nation magazine, according to Oxford Dictionaries.

"Given that usage of the term hasn't shown any signs of slowing down, I wouldn't be surprised if 'post-truth' becomes one of the defining words of our time," said Grathwohl.

Indeed. This type of campaigning is nothing new. President Kennedy's 1960 ad attacking Richard Nixon was one of the first. President Eisenhower said when asked if Vice President Nixon had provided him with any major ideas he had utilized, "If you give me a week, I might think of one. I don't remember."

It was a classic template for today's attack ads, which are the clear majority of political ads now placed in various media. The ad did not focus on any actual decisions made by Nixon in his career. The ad was designed to elicit an emotional reaction: If President Eisenhower didn't get any useful advice from him, how good could Nixon be?

Attack ads are designed to wage a personal attack against an opposing candidate or political party to gain support for the attacking candidate and attract voters. An attack ad will generally unfairly criticize an opponent's political platform, usually by pointing out its faults. Often the ad will simply make use of innuendo, based on opposition research.

But today's post-truth politics put the early attack ads to shame. Independent Journal Review published this list of lies told by Hillary Clinton during her presidential campaign:[30]

- "I am the only candidate who ran in either the Democratic or Republican primary who said from the very beginning (that) I will not raise taxes on the middle class."

- "Back in the Great Recession, when millions of jobs across America hung in the balance, Donald Trump said rescuing the auto industry didn't really matter very much."
- "(FBI Director) Comey said my answers were truthful, and what I've said is consistent with what I have told the American people."
- "I was gone (when Obama drew the red line in Syria.)"
- "I'm the only candidate in the Democratic primary, or actually on either side, who Wall Street financiers and hedge fund managers are actually running ads against."
- "The only two (Donald Trump tax returns) we have show that he hasn't paid a penny in taxes."
- "We are now, for the first time ever, energy independent."
- "(Donald Trump) wants us to pull out of NATO."
- "(Donald Trump) doesn't make a thing in America."
- "I do think there is an agenda out there, supported by my opponent, to (privatize the VA)."
- "Mike Pence slashed education funding in Indiana."
- "Let me repeat what I have repeated for many months now. I never received nor sent any material that was marked classified."
- "(My personal email server) was allowed."
- "(Donald Trump) has been talking about the option of using a nuclear weapon against our Western European allies."
- "I don't think (Bernie Sanders has) had a single negative ad ever run against him."
- "Our campaign depends on small donations for the majority of our support."

- "If I had not asked for my emails all to be made public, none of this would have been in the public arena."
- "You are three times more likely to be able to get a mortgage if you're a white applicant than if you're black or Hispanic, even if you have the same credentials."
- "We now have more jobs in solar than we do in oil."
- "What I have put forward does not add a penny to the debt."
- "Not a single Republican candidate, announced or potential, is clearly and consistently supporting a path to citizenship. Not one."
- "Donald Trump says he'd deport 16 million people."
- "I am the only candidate on either side who has laid out a specific plan about what I would do to defeat ISIS."
- "Every piece of legislation, just about, that I ever introduced had a Republican co-sponsor."
- "We now have driven (health care) costs down to the lowest they've been in 50 years."
- "(The gun industry is) the only business in America that is wholly protected from any kind of liability."
- "Not one of the 17 GOP candidates has discussed how they'd address the rising cost of college."
- "Hedge fund managers themselves make more and pay less in taxes than nurses and truck drivers."
- "All my grandparents, you know, (immigrated) over here."

Of course, Trump had his own list of falsehoods:[31]

- President Obama lied about his birth certificate
- Hillary Clinton started "Birtherism"
- Obama wears an "Arabic" ring

- Obama was born "Barry Soetero"
- Climate change is a hoax, created by China to undermine U.S. manufacturing
- Rafael Cruz, father of Ted Cruz, was linked to the Kennedy Assassination
- Obama founded ISIS
- After a protester attempted to rush the stage at a Trump rally in March, Trump claimed that the demonstrator had "ties to ISIS," citing a hoax video that mocked the man.
- Muslims celebrated 9/11 in New Jersey
- San Bernardino attackers' neighbors knew of their plot
- Syrian refugees come to the U.S. without vetting
- In June 2016, Trump said that Clinton "wants to spend hundreds of billions to resettle Middle Eastern refugees in the United States." The AP pointed out that "the entire U.S. budget for refugee resettlement is less than $1.2 billion a year."
- At two different campaign events, Trump claimed that Clinton, if elected president, would allow 650 million people to "pour in" and "triple the size of our country in one week."
- Trump has accused Clinton of making a "radical call for open borders, meaning anyone in the world can enter the United States without any limit at all."
- Countries like Mexico send criminals to the U.S.
- Cities like Oakland, California and Ferguson, Missouri, are among the most dangerous in the world.
- White people are mostly killed by black people
- In a desperate attempt to justify his voter fraud scare, Trump said that Mitt Romney and John McCain each

"got zero votes" in the city of Philadelphia when they ran for president.

- Trump accused fire marshals of wrongly turning away people from his rallies for political reasons, wondering if they are Democrats. As it turns out, the Trump campaign agreed on attendance caps for safety reasons with the very local fire departments that he criticized.
- Hillary Clinton wants to end religious liberty
- Trump responded to the outcry over his Trump University scam by insisting that the Better Business Bureau gave it an "A" rating; instead, the BBB noted that Trump U received a "D-" rating in its final year. After the so-called university closed in 2010, its score rose on the BBB's website because complaints from the time it was functioning expired.
- He authored the best-selling business book of all time
- I never said climate change was a hoax
- I never said John McCain wasn't a hero
- I never said I have a relationship with Putin; in 2013, Trump told MSNBC, "I do have a relationship with him. He's done a very brilliant job in terms of what he represents and who he's representing."
- I never mocked a disabled reporter
- I never said China should face a 45 percent tariff; in audio posted by the New York Times, Trump said he would tax products coming in from China: "I would do a tax and let me tell you what the tax should be. The tax should be 45 percent."
- I never said Megyn Kelly should be removed from the debate; just days before denying that he asked for Kelly to be excluded from the debate, Trump tweeted that Kelly "should not be allowed" to moderate the forum.

- I never said I was perfect; in 2014, Trump wrote, "I consider myself too perfect and have no faults."
- I saw Michelle Obama attack Hillary Clinton
- I saw the Iran money transfer; on at least two occasions, Trump insisted that he watched a nonexistent "tape" of a money transfer between the U.S. and Iran. But in an almost unprecedented move, Trump eventually admitted the tape didn't show a money transfer.

Clearly, politicians and elected officials have been skirting the truth since the beginning of contested elections. But we have now reached the point where literally everything the candidates and now the president says needs to be checked. And when it is checked, and falsehoods are detected, a significant percentage of the population and electorate doesn't even care.

If it's a Democrat caught in a lie, the conservative media will jump all over it, and those of Democratic / liberal mindset will brush it off by saying that it's all manufactured by that "right-wing conspiracy," to quote one famous characterization.

Likewise, if someone points out a falsehood by a Republican / conservative or Trump, it will immediately be dismissed or "spun" by the conservative media.

Pew Research reported in 2016 that 39 percent of people polled called themselves Independents, with 32 percent calling themselves Democrats and 23 percent saying they are Republicans.[32] But even most of the self-labeled Independents usually vote for one party or the other, Pew reported.

It is then fair to say that most U.S. adults have a definite political persuasion, and a high likelihood of having selective exposure influence how they filter reports about specific candidates. The minority of people who don't have a strong affiliation with any political party or mindset likely throw up their hands in disbelief at what masquerades as qualified candidates and legitimate political arguments currently.

Post-truth is a very true description of our current political culture. It represents the convergence of societal factors and trends into a perfect storm:

- With the incredible amount of media choices available, media consumers are more likely to find a source that jives with their personal beliefs and interests, thereby appealing to their selective exposure predisposition;
- The news media, whose primary role is as watchdog over government, has reached all-time lows regarding the percentage of Americans who believe them;
- The media that have the highest approval numbers (a.k.a., ratings) are the politically leaning outlets. Therefore, the information presented there is a magnet for the people for whom selective exposure is strong;
- Social media has spawned hundreds of very niche-oriented sites that further enable information consumers to find not only what information they are seeking, but also from which perspective.

Because the news media has lost the respect of the American public, the candidates follow suit. When John F. Kennedy and Richard Nixon participated in the first nationally televised presidential debate, the candidates answered questions that were posed to them by the moderators. As the decades have passed and the media is no longer respected, it basically is a free-for-all nowadays. It was interesting to watch the 2016 presidential debates, highlighted by the two candidates never answering a question directly, and by the moderators losing control on several occasions.

Our national political structure and culture is built on Republican and Democratic candidates who tell their very devoted bases what they want to hear, whether it is true or not. Distrust is rampant in the media and in people who don't share one's personal selective exposure.

It will take a very bold individual, with like-minded supporters, to begin the reversal of this culture. It will take someone who will tell the truth to the American people – in particular, to those whose selective exposure has not shut out all ideas other than the ones to which they have attached themselves.

The gauntlet facing our ideal candidate

Every person reading this book has a unique mental image of the qualities of a good president or presidential candidate. So, let's make clear that an ideal candidate, from the author's perspective, is someone who:

- Places a higher priority on solving the nation's problems than partisan politics
- Will nominate appointees based on qualifications and experience rather than political patronage
- Has demonstrable achievements in managing large organizations
- Listens to all perspectives and does not let his or her natural tendency toward selective exposure disqualify some ideas
- Believes the electorate should be addressed with respect, as an employee would address a superior
- Believes the electorate should be told the truth about the situations in which the country finds itself (excluding classified information)

- Believes his or her contributions to creating a better nation supersede goals of personal financial gain
- Has natural leadership qualities, including:
  - Focus
  - Confidence
  - Transparency
  - Integrity
  - Inspiration
  - Passion
  - Innovation
  - Patience
  - Stoicism
  - Decisiveness
  - Personable
  - Positivity
  - Generosity
  - Persistence
  - Accountability

The person who meets all the standards above is out there somewhere in the United States. We'll keep track of this person throughout the rest of the book with the name Pat. (Remember the androgynous character from Saturday Night Live? Our Pat does not look like that Julia Sweeney character, but has a name that could be either a man or woman.)

Why has Pat not yet made a run for public office or even president? Impeding our would-be ideal president is a gauntlet that would stop King Kong, Godzilla, Gandhi or Superman in his tracks.

Impediment #1: The onslaught of media – social and mainstream – that dig into every crevasse of each candidate's life history looking for dirt

We all make mistakes and have screw-ups in our lives. If a candidate has even one major screw-up in his history, there is no avoiding having it thrown in his face for the remainder of not only the campaign but for the rest of his life. If he slips and shows humanity by uttering a curse word near any microphone, it's over.

If you have made one regrettable mistake in your life that any other person is aware of, that person could potentially tell that story either on social media or to a reporter. The same is true if it appears in a police report, court document, or even a hand-written note that somebody you had forgotten completely about held on to for years and years.

Not only must the would-be candidate think of herself, but she also must think of her family. Does her family deserve to be embarrassed or even humiliated because of a stupid mistake she made when she was probably much younger?

In 2016, Bill Kristol, editor of the conservative *Weekly Standard*, tried to recruit an alternative to Donald Trump. The Bloomberg Politics website reported that Kristol considered David French, a *National Review* writer and Harvard-educated lawyer who served in Iraq and earned a Bronze Star.[33] Despite being almost entirely unknown to the public, French seemingly would be regarded as the sort of idealistic, accomplished, upstanding, citizen who should try his hand at electoral politics – or at least so Kristol may have believed.

So, what happened? Without any confirmation from French — and without even waiting for Kristol to confirm that he was trying to urge French to run — the Washington political establishment started digging for dirt.

Almost immediately Politico.com reporter Kevin Robillard discovered a 2011 column summarizing a book written by French and his wife, Nancy, about their separation while he was in Iraq. The book discussed how they maintained a long-distance relationship during wartime. The couple agreed, among other things, that Nancy would restrict her phone and email contacts with men and stay off Facebook. Robillard summarized the column — apparently without reading the book — as saying that French "wouldn't let his wife email men or use Facebook."

Never mind that French, if he had run, would have faced a man married three times who avoided wartime military service, and the wife of a former president who did the same while subjecting the nation to its most spectacular sex scandal. Never mind the experience of people who have had to deal with the strains that modern combat service places on a marriage. Never mind that French's wife is also a writer and co-author of the book, not merely a passive participant in her marriage. Nobody asked her.

The 24/7 social and legacy media will consume anyone who dares to be sincere and candid in public. Knowing this, it is not a bit surprising that our ideal candidate has not yet stepped forward.

The media also seized on the fact that French writes *National Review*'s recaps for the "Game of Thrones" TV series — criticized as a sign of how preposterous his not-yet-announced run would surely be, how low would be his chances of success. Couldn't Bill Kristol find someone better, the pundits wanted to know? Was it so ridiculous to imagine a TV reviewer in the Oval Office, when we would elect a reality TV star instead?

French, in a way, is a member of the media, but that didn't save him. The fraternity didn't stop reporters from churning out instant opposition research at the mere rumor that French might be considering higher office. They turned on their own.

Syndicated columnist Cal Thomas put it best:[34]

> Occasionally I am asked if I ever considered running for political office. My response: "I did once, but I took two aspirin, lay down for a while and the feeling went away."
>
> Besides not wanting to accept a pay cut, why would I want to put myself through the agony of exposing the smallest misdeed and bad decision to political opponents and a ravenous media who could turn my public image into something no family member would recognize? Not to mention the amount of money I would have to raise that would go up exponentially the higher the office sought. With each donated dollar a little piece of my soul, character and integrity must ultimately be exchanged. Why else do people donate if they don't expect something in return? Might that something somehow dilute whatever virtues I am perceived to possess?

What I have just described are major reasons why people who might be smart and capable enough to run for office decline the "honor."

Why does the media do this? Remember our discussion earlier in the book about each media entity's financial need to be first, and the fact that sensationalism sells. Media consumers will stop and watch or click on something they haven't seen before. There is no question that the free press's role in our society is as a watchdog over government. But that role has been contorted to a form of gossip column in some cases.

Most news organizations' staffs are so diminished these days that real investigative journalism is almost a non-entity. If you saw the movie, "Spotlight," about the sexual abuse scandal in the Catholic archdiocese of Boston, you'll remember that the *Boston Globe* had at least five staff members assigned to that story over a period of several months.

Fifteen years after that investigative masterpiece, there are few if any media companies that have the budget for staff to investigate stories to that extent. Most news reports these days focus on what people said, or recitations of press releases, not on the investigation of records and documents.

A common cliché in the newspaper business is that today's edition of the paper is the "Daily Miracle." Staffers will joke that the publication of another daily newspaper was nothing short of a miracle, with the paucity of staff and resources available now compared to even just 10 to 15 years ago.

Media these days also don't hesitate to publish or air allegations that come from anonymous sources, another strike against would-be candidate Pat. Despite meeting the list of attributes listed above, Pat must decide if he or she wants one or two mistakes in the past to be fodder for hundreds, if not thousands, of media outlets desperate for views and clicks.

Obstacle #2: the cost

It's incredibly expensive to run for president. Clinton and Trump spent nearly $1.8 billion between them in the 2016 race. Clinton spent the most, at more than $1.1 billion.[35]

To get that kind of money, you need to be connected to very wealthy people who will bankroll your campaign. (Most of us don't have those sorts of connections.) And someone making that level of donation will want to see some return on investment. That means kissing goodbye the listening-to-all-perspectives attribute. You will be beholden to the wants and needs of your financial supporters.

Much of the money raised for both candidates came from existing political party entities and Super PACs, also known as political action committees. The Super PAC money does not pass through a candidate's accounts, because Super PACs, by law, are not allowed to have consultation or contact with the candidates they support. (wink, wink)

On top of the $1.8 billion spent by the candidates, another $1.1 billion was spent by Super PACs.[36] Running for president is a multi-billion-dollar endeavor. In our current system, the people who will emerge from both parties are flush with cash themselves and have the connections through which to raise hundreds of millions more.

"To discover who rules, follow the gold," is the argument of author Thomas Ferguson in his 1995 book, "Golden Rule," a history of modern American politics. The role big money plays in defining political outcomes has long been obvious to ordinary Americans, but most pundits and scholars have virtually dismissed this assumption, Ferguson argues.

Even with skyrocketing campaign costs, the belief that major financial interests primarily determine who parties nominate and where they stand on the issues — in effect, Democrats and Republicans are merely the left and right wings of the "Property Party" — has been ignored by most political scientists, according to Ferguson.[37] Of course, it is evident to most people that the Golden Rule very much applies to U.S. politics at all levels.

Impediment #3: a slew of state laws meant to keep Americans who are not Democrats or Republicans from threatening the two existing major parties

These laws prevent rivals from emerging that might replace the existing parties—the way the Republicans replaced the Whigs over the issue of slavery.

Unlike Democrats or Republicans, independents and third parties must fight their way onto the ballot in all 50 states. That takes money and boots on the ground. Even with both, an independent candidate will meet immediate obstacles from state laws and interpretations by local officials who are themselves typically stalwarts of the "big two" parties. These officials will challenge signatures on nomination petitions themselves and even the eligibility of those who collected them. During Ralph Nader's 2004 presidential campaign, a

Pennsylvania lawyer for the Democratic Party successfully invalidated the authenticity of over 30,000 of Nader's signatures — often for silly reasons like someone signing "Bill" instead of "William."[38]

Political historian Richard Hofstadter said in his 1955 book "The Age of Reform: Bryan to F.D.R.," "Third parties are like bees: once they have stung, they die. ... (Third parties') function has not been to win or govern, but to agitate, educate, generate new ideas, and supply the dynamic element in our political life. When a third party's demands become popular enough, they are appropriated by one or both major parties, and the third party disappears."

Parties can only receive public funding for the general election if they earned at least five percent of the popular vote in the last presidential election. Since the end of World War II, third party tickets have only achieved that feat twice. Neither the Libertarian nor the Green party did so in 2016. Such a high threshold for public support serves the purpose of preventing third parties from breaking through to compete. Third parties can't get a foothold in an election without money, and they can't get money unless they do well in an election.

Independent presidential candidates typically must petition each state to have their names printed on the general election ballot. For the 2016 presidential contest, estimates showed an independent candidate would need to collect more than 880,000 petition signatures to appear on the general election ballot in every state. Think about the chances of accomplishing that without some organized group's help.

An individual can run as a write-in candidate. In 33 states, a write-in candidate must file some paperwork before the election. In nine states, write-in voting for presidential candidates is not allowed. The remaining states do not require write-in candidates to file paperwork in advance of the election.

Some states prohibit candidates who sought and failed to secure the nomination of a political party from running as independents in the general election.

Early ballot deadlines in some states prevent independent candidates from emerging after it becomes apparent that the choices presented by the two primary parties are opposed by so many. In Texas, for example, the 2016 deadline for third-party filings fell before the Democratic and Republican primaries were complete.

An organization calling itself Better For America emerged during the 2016 campaign with a goal of eliminating these obstacles to a third-party or independent candidate.

BFA's website said the organization believed there was still time for someone with integrity, honor, and trustworthiness to compete against the two major party candidates.

But, a message on the group's website dated August 23, 2016 said:[39]

> After months of working to provide ballot access and recruit a presidential candidate worthy of this moment for our country, today Better For America announces an end to its candidate recruitment and ballot access efforts. BFA continues to call for leadership to

> address the current political crisis, and will
> pursue litigation to make this pathway
> possible.

Like independent candidates, this non-aligned political group apparently found the obstacles too daunting.

Impediment #4: the lengthy process

It begins years before the next election. Potential candidates and their supporters make it known through various unofficial means that the individual is thinking about a run for the White House. That begins the process of taking the temperature of public interest and support through various formal and informal methods.

Then, the would-be candidate puts together an "exploratory committee" to explore the possibility of a run for the presidency. At some point after that, the candidate makes the announcement official.

Then the campaign begins in full force, first for the party's nomination across the 50 states in primary elections and caucuses. If that is successful, the national race is on for six to seven months.

This helps to explain why people who don't earn income from politics don't venture down this road very often. Individuals who have jobs or family considerations just can't do it. You must be available 365 days a year, sometimes making several stops in several states in the same day. It's exhausting, and the process does not generate any income for day-to-day existence.

Obstacle #5: the salary

Companies in our capitalistic society compete to attract the best and brightest employees through various means, including pay and benefits. Frankly, the U.S. president's salary pales in comparison to what upper managers at the nation's large corporations earn.

A 2001 Congressional act raised the presidential salary to $400,000 per year, with a $50,000 annual expense account, a $100,000 non-taxable travel account, and $19,000 for entertainment. We have no official statistics, but it's not beyond the realm of comprehension that President Trump blew through those expense accounts within weeks or months of his inauguration. Not that he needs them. After all, he said after he was elected that he wasn't taking the $400,000 salary, which might be seen at first blush as a consideration toward easing the taxpayers' burden just a bit.

But the Founding Fathers felt it important that the president accept the salary, so that it was clear that the president was working for the people instead of for his own interests. They put George Washington's salary at $25,000, an enormous amount for that period in history. He initially declined it but reversed that position after pressure from the Congress.

Trump's potential benefits of being president potentially dwarf the $400,000 salary. For example, he has the power to appoint the IRS chief overseeing his tax audit, and the National Labor Relations Board members who rule on union-busting efforts at his casinos. Business lobbyists could give Trump or his children stock in return for favorable treatment, and the public would have no way of knowing. This is not an accusation, but an example of potential financial benefits that could far outweigh salary. It is also a look into the mindset of the Founding Fathers when they pressured Washington to accept his salary.

Herbert Hoover declined his presidential salary due to his lucrative interests in mining. He donated his salary to charity, as did John F. Kennedy, who was born into considerable wealth and lived off a sizeable trust fund.

Washington's $25,000 salary would be between $450,000 and $500,000 in today's dollars. Trump's would-be salary is comparable in 21st-century dollars to what Washington made back in the late 1700s. What is to motivate our best and brightest to leave positions in corporate America, take a huge pay cut, and subject themselves to the whims of a broken Congress?

This is not to say that the only people who are viable candidates are corporate bigwigs. But in some cases, the personality and integrity traits possessed by Pat could belong to someone whose intelligence, creativity and management skills have propelled her to a position in which a corporation was happy to compensate her at a very high level. Along with the other obstacles listed above, the pay for the office of president is not at all commensurate with the time put in, the amount of responsibility, and the level of stress endured.

By comparison, a first-year Major League Baseball player makes a minimum of $555,000. That number has increased substantially as the value of baseball entertainment has skyrocketed in recent decades. While nobody buys tickets to watch the president in action, it's time for a comprehensive review of the salary structure for the president and other federal elected officials. If your salary is seven figures, you might be much less inclined to take risks with taxpayer dollars that could result in you losing your job. It would never be a popular move among the electorate, but it's time that presidential compensation is enough to attract the best and brightest for the spoils of the salary and benefits, rather than the spoils of lobbyists and political patronage.

In 1888, James Bryce wrote "The American Commonwealth," in which he gave three reasons why great men don't become president:

> Great men rarely go into politics;
> The political process is not designed for great men to succeed; and,
> Except in times of crisis, great men are not needed in the presidency.

Our country is in a political crisis which members of the political parties in power are not motivated to fix. The United States just completed a presidential election in which the candidates nominated by the Republican and Democratic parties were wholly unsuitable. We need a great man or woman to step forward and face the gauntlet described in this chapter.

Pat will likely also face the very daunting task of running a presidential campaign without millions or billions of his or her own dollars.

Follow the money

"Follow the money" is a catchphrase popularized by the 1976 drama-documentary motion picture "All The President's Men." The classic movie portrayed the efforts of journalists Bob Woodward and Carl Bernstein to investigate the truth behind the break-in at the Watergate hotel.

For the film, screenwriter William Goldman attributed the phrase to Woodward and Bernstein's unnamed source, "Deep Throat." However, the phrase did not appear in the non-fiction book of the same name, nor in any documentation of the scandal.

The book does say, "The key was the secret campaign cash, and it should all be traced," which Woodward says to Senator Sam Ervin, chairman of the Senate Select Committee to Investigate Campaign Practices — known more popularly as the "Ervin Committee" or the "Watergate Committee." It's possible that screenwriters condensed Woodward's statement to the phrase "follow the money."

Since then, "follow the money" has frequently been used in investigative journalism and political debate.

In September 2016, the Trump campaign used the phrase to criticize Hillary Clinton and the Clinton Foundation. In February 2017, Bernstein used the phrase to encourage reporters to discover President Trump's potential conflicts of interest.

In a 2015 campaign interview, Trump – addressing why he had donated to candidates on both sides of the political aisle over his business career — verbally illustrated the impact of money in election campaigns by donors.[40]

> "Look, politicians are all talk, they're no action. They don't do the job, they don't know what they're doing. I know them better than anybody. I deal with all of them. And, you know, I make contributions to many of them. They're friends, they're this. It's smart. It's called being an intelligent person and a great business person. ... But the truth is that, you have to be able to get along with—if you're gonna be a business person, even in the United States, you wanna get along with all sides because you're gonna need things from everybody. And you wanna get along with all sides, it's very important."

Clearly, in the Post-Truth Era of presidential politics and long before, candidates need money to run campaigns, for the reasons outlined earlier in the book. As Trump pointed out in his quote, businesspeople understand campaign donations buy influence. The more money you give, the more influence you buy.

This is a primary reason Pat faces such an uphill battle. He or she would have to accept donations from business interests which elicit the unwritten expectation of the return on political favor when needed. The question frustrated candidates have been pondering for years is:

How do we reduce the need for and influence of money in presidential campaigns?

In 2010, The United States Supreme Court ruled in a 5–4 vote that freedom of speech prohibited the government from restricting independent political expenditures by a nonprofit corporation. For-profit corporations, labor unions, and other associations received the same benefit.

In the case, the conservative non-profit organization Citizens United wanted to air a film critical of Hillary Clinton. The group also wanted to advertise the film during television broadcasts shortly before the 2008 Democratic presidential primary election, in which Clinton was running.

Citizens United sought an injunction against the Federal Election Commission in the United States District Court for the District of Columbia to prevent the application of the Bipartisan Campaign Reform Act (BCRA) to its film "Hillary: The Movie." The film expressed opinions about whether Senator Hillary Rodham Clinton would make a good president.

To regulate "big money" campaign contributions, the BCRA applies a variety of restrictions to "electioneering communications." Section 203 of the BCRA prevents corporations or labor unions from funding such communication from their general treasuries. Sections 201 and

311 require the disclosure of donors to such communication and a disclaimer when the communication is not authorized by the candidate it intends to support.

The court found the provisions of the law that prohibited corporations and unions from making such electioneering communications conflicted with the U.S. Constitution.

In effect, the Supreme Court ruled that corporations had the same rights of freedom of speech as individuals. The fact that corporations typically have significantly more financial means to express their political views than individuals was not a consideration in the ruling. This led to the creation of the Super PACs that fund a huge portion of presidential campaigns, as well as campaigns for and against other national issues.

The case did not affect the federal ban on direct contributions from corporations or unions to candidate campaigns or political parties, which is why Super PACs are, by statute, not allowed to communicate directly with campaigns they support. (wink, wink, wink)

On April 2, 2014, the Supreme Court issued a 5-4 ruling that the 1971 Federal Elections Campaign Act's aggregate limits restricting how much money a donor may contribute in total to all candidates or committees violated the First Amendment. This further opened the gates for individuals and corporations with deep pockets to donate without any legislative limits.

The *New York Times* reported in October 2015 that then, only 158 families, along with companies they own or control, had contributed $176 million – or nearly half of the money raised to that point — in the first phase of the presidential campaign.

Maryland Democrat John Sarbanes introduced H.R. 20, the Government by the People Act, described as a leading Democratic congressional proposal to level the playing field. The bill, which died after the 114th Congress did not enact it, would have given every citizen a voucher worth up to $50 through a "My Voice Tax Credit" for campaign contributions in $5 increments. It also would have aimed to make small donations as influential as large donations by matching any donation on a six-to-one level through the establishment of a Freedom From Influence Fund.

"We know that if the role of money in our elections were reduced and the level of civility in our politics increased, the result would be the election of more women, more minorities, more young people and more people dedicated to serving the public interest, not special interests," Sarbanes and House Minority Leader Nancy Pelosi (D-California) wrote. "Most members of Congress would leap at the chance to fund their campaigns without having to turn to a familiar cast of big donors and entrenched interests. Today, that's virtually impossible."

Republicans contended the bill would have amounted to government funding of private speech, plus that it would have contributed to levels of unsustainable government spending. Sarbanes's bill didn't come up for a vote in the GOP-controlled Congress.

Another bill, The Fair Elections Now Act, had similar provisions but would have also allowed candidates to raise unlimited donations provided they did not individually exceed $150. The idea was to level the playing field for candidates who can demonstrate a minimum degree of support while also helping to free up incumbent members of Congress from the burden of spending hours each day fundraising rather than working on legislation or helping their constituents. That bill also did not come up for a vote in the 114th Congress, which lasted from January 2015 through January 2017.

For many years, presidential campaigns received a significant percentage of their funding from public sources. The presidential election campaign fund checkoff appears on U.S. income tax return forms as the question, "Do you want $3 of your federal tax to go to the Presidential Election Campaign Fund?"

Originally $1 and implemented in the 1970s as an attempt at the public funding of elections, this money provides for the financing of presidential primary and general election campaigns. Beginning with the 1973 tax year, individual taxpayers could designate $1 to be applied to the Presidential Election Campaign Fund. Both the Republican and Democratic nominees for the general election receive a fixed amount of checkoff dollars.

Nominees from other political parties may qualify for a smaller, proportionate amount of checkoff funds if they receive over five percent of the vote. Matching funds are also given for primary candidates for small contributions. The campaign fund is designed to reduce a candidate's dependence on large contributions from individuals and special-interest groups. This program is administered by the Federal Election Commission (FEC).

Requirements to be declared eligible include agreeing to an overall spending limit, abiding by spending limits in each state, using public funds only for legitimate campaign-related expenses, keeping financial records and permitting an extensive campaign audit. The last time any presidential candidate accepted the federal funds (and corresponding spending limit) was John McCain in 2008.

Checking the box does not change the amount of an individual's tax or refund. Three dollars of an individual's tax is diverted to a different government budget line item than it might have been otherwise.

Perhaps because Americans hear how much money is flowing into campaigns from corporate donors, the number of people checking the tax return box to donate has fallen drastically. In 1979, nearly 29 percent of taxpayers donated. By tax year 2015, the number had fallen to 5.4 percent.

Through October 2016, the Presidential Election Campaign Fund maintained by the Federal Elections Commissions had more than $317 million available for use by candidates. Here's how to qualify for the use of those funds, according to the FEC:

PRIMARY MATCHING FUNDS

Partial public funding is available to Presidential primary candidates in the form of matching payments. The federal government will match up to $250 of an individual's total contributions to an eligible candidate. Only candidates seeking nomination by a political party to the office of President are eligible to receive primary matching funds. In addition, a candidate must establish eligibility by showing broad-based public support. He or she must raise in excess of $5,000 in each of at least 20 states (i.e., over $100,000). Although an individual may contribute up to $2,700 to a primary candidate, only a maximum of $250 per individual applies toward the $5,000 threshold in each state.

Candidates also must agree to:
• Limit campaign spending for all primary elections to $10 million plus a cost-of-living adjustment (COLA). This is called the national spending limit.
• Limit campaign spending in each state to $200,000 plus COLA, or to a specified amount based on the number of voting age individuals in the state (plus COLA), whichever is greater.
• Limit spending from personal funds to $50,000.

Once they have established eligibility for matching payments, Presidential candidates may receive public funds to match contributions from individual contributors, up to $250 per individual.

Because candidates receive many non-matchable contributions, such as those from political committees, they generally raise more money than they receive in matching funds.

GENERAL ELECTION FUNDING

The Presidential nominee of each major party may become eligible for a public grant of $20 million (plus a cost-of-living adjustment) for campaigning in the general election. To be eligible to receive the public funds, the candidate must limit spending to the amount of the grant and may not accept private contributions for the campaign. Private contributions may, however, be accepted for a special account maintained exclusively to pay for legal and accounting expenses associated with complying with the campaign finance law. These legal and accounting expenses are not subject to the expenditure limit.

In addition, candidates may spend up to $50,000 from their own personal funds. Such spending does not count against the expenditure limit.

Minor party candidates and new party candidates may become eligible for partial public funding of their general election campaigns. (A minor party candidate is the nominee of a party whose candidate received between 5 and 25 percent of the total popular vote in the preceding Presidential election. A new party candidate is the nominee of a party that is neither a major party nor a minor party.) The amount of public funding to which a minor party candidate is entitled is based on the ratio of the party's popular vote in the preceding Presidential election to the average popular vote of the two major party candidates in that election. A new party candidate receives partial public funding after the election if he/she receives 5 percent or more of the vote. The entitlement is based on the ratio of the new party candidate's popular vote in the current election to the average popular vote of the two major party candidates in the election.

Although minor and new party candidates may supplement public funds with private contributions and may exempt some fundraising costs from their expenditure limit, they are otherwise subject to the same spending limit and other requirements that apply to major party candidates.

So, there are some financial options for Pat. But the sad truth is that, as mentioned earlier, the system is stacked to benefit the big two parties. It's been more than eight years since any candidate was willing to agree to the spending limits required to receive the FEC funds. They all know that the donations they'll receive from big-spending individuals, once combined with the money corporations donate to Super PACs, will be hundreds or thousands of times more than the public funding system.

Campaign finance reform advocates say that the $3 check-off still offers an important symbolic outlet for voters to express their support for a better campaign finance system.

Common Cause Senior Policy Counsel Stephen Spaulding told ThinkProgress.org that the presidential public financing was a resounding success for 20 years and could be again if Congress would act to make more public funds available to candidates.[41]

"There is a way to do it, and it wouldn't be that hard. All that is to say, when people do their tax returns, they're reminded 'there's that check-off box' that can remind people that public financing is a better way to do things, empower voters, and reset priorities."

"Rather than throw the baby out with the bathwater, let's fix the system," he urged. "(Citizens) should check the box and show that it matters, there's still an appetite."

There is indeed an appetite to fix the system. But the people with that hunger often feel unheard due to the high volume and frequency of messages coming from the extreme left and extreme right which control today's political messaging.

Democrats, Republicans have self-sorted

As our social and political cultures have changed rapidly over the past few decades, one of the more obvious differences is the diminished civility of contested elections — and political discussion in general.

James Thurber, University Distinguished Professor of Government and Founder and Director of the Center for Congressional and Presidential Studies at American University, points out the following in his book, "American Gridlock: The Sources, Character and Impact of Political Polarization:"[42]

Representatives in Congress respond more to their activist bases than to the median voter in the general election. This "force for polarization" means that both independent voters and members who reach across the aisle and compromise are nearly extinct.

The electorate's growing partisan nature has coincided with a high degree of consistency in the results of recent elections.

The 2012 presidential election saw the highest party loyalty in the history of the American National Election Study (conducted since 1948): 93 percent of Democrats voted for Obama and 93 percent of Republicans voted for Romney. The 2012 election also produced the lowest rate of ticket splitting, as 90 percent of Americans supported the same party for President and the House, 89 percent for President and the Senate, and 87 percent for the House and the Senate.

Voters are less inclined to support a centrist candidate than ever before, Thurber claims, and the widening gap is staggering as shown in the battle for the presidential nomination in 2016. Candidates have more reason to appeal to their extreme supporters than to try to win independent voters as a pragmatic moderate.

Commonly we hear the term political polarization to describe this change. But others say the cause is what is known as political sorting.

Polarization is the erosion of the political center as citizens move to the extremes. But that is not what has happened in the United States, according to Morris Fiorina, the Wendt Family Professor of Political Science at Stanford University and a Senior Fellow at the Hoover Institution. He has published numerous works on the sorting phenomenon and says the center of the American electorate is still there.

Via political sorting, Fiorina says, the Democrats are a more homogeneously liberal party and the Republicans a more homogeneously conservative party compared to the 1970s, for example.[43]

Particular values receive defense from only one of the two sides, and specific kinds of people seem to get a sympathetic hearing by only one of the two parties. The consequence is that the actions considered by government bodies are more likely to present stark choices today than in some earlier, less polarized, more civil eras. Therefore, elections matter more. As the stakes rise, civility falls.

While the lack of politeness and courtesy is very evident, it is not nearly as big of a problem as others we have outlined. These include outright lying, a government that cares little about true and false and right and wrong, and an electorate that no longer trusts the entity that is supposed to be their government watchdog, the free press.

Jim Webb, who was running for the Democratic presidential nomination in 2015, dropped out of the race. In his announcement, he blasted the two parties and suggested that the real political force in America is independents.

"Our political candidates are being pulled to the extremes," he said, at the National Press Club in Washington. "They are increasingly out of step with the people they are supposed to serve. Poll after poll shows that a strong plurality of Americans is neither Republican nor Democrat. Overwhelmingly they're independents. Americans don't like the extremes to which both parties have moved in recent years, and I don't blame them."

Recent numbers confirm Webb's claim. A Gallup poll in early 2017 showed political independents continue to outnumber Democrats and Republicans in the U.S. by a significant margin. While the percentage of independents fell in the presidential election year, as it often does, it remains higher than it was in the 1990s and 2000s.

An average of 39 percent of Americans self-identified as political independents in 2016, Gallup said, down from 42 percent in 2015 and reaching its lowest point in six years.[44]

Separately, Gallup found that Americans continue to give higher unfavorable than favorable ratings to both parties, which had not been the case until 2010. Frustration with the way the government is functioning — particularly the partisan gridlock that seemingly prevents the federal government from addressing major issues facing the country — may be a catalyst of that feeling.

Joe Biden announced shortly after Webb's declaration that he would forgo a presidential run, and he made a similar case that America is being damaged by excessive partisanship.

"I believe that we have to end the divisive partisan politics that is ripping this country apart," Biden said, in remarks in the Rose Garden. "And I think we can. It's mean-spirited, it's petty, and it's gone on for much too long. I don't believe, like some do, that it's naïve to talk to Republicans. I don't think we should look at Republicans as our enemies. They are our opposition. They're not our enemies. And for the sake of the country, we must work together. As the president has said many times, compromise is not a dirty word. But look at it this way, folks: How does this country function without consensus? How can we move forward without being able to arrive at consensus? Four more years of this kind of pitched battle may be more than this country can take. We have to change it. We have to change it."

As a reader of this book, you are evidence that a center still exists. Many "politically sorted" people who see from the title that the book does not side specifically with either the left or the right will react to their selective exposure instincts and dismiss it. Many experts say that the effect of sorting is much more evident among those who are politicians or politically active than those who are not. In fact, political sorting and selective exposure are intimately intertwined.

If our elected officials, politicians, and politically active citizens remain in opposite corners ready only for battle, the result when they emerge from their sides will always be a flailing exchange of words and deeds. Somehow, the two political parties need to emerge from their corners with open minds and ears instead of boxing gloves raised.

While the factors causing this political sorting are new, the condition of dividing up politically goes as far back in our history as our second president, John Adams, who wrote, "There is nothing which I dread so much as a division of the republic into two great parties, each arranged under its leader, and concerting measures in opposition to each other. This, in my humble apprehension, is to be dreaded as the greatest political evil under our Constitution."

Because there are only two parties represented in our Congressional houses, there is an ultra-high likelihood that one party will have a numbers advantage over the other regarding seats (and corresponding votes). The need and desire for cooperation between the parties continue to diminish.

The Norwegian government has eight represented parties in its congress, known as the Storting, and none of the eight has a majority on its own. Therefore, there is much incentive for cooperation and compromise to get things accomplished.

Obviously, the Democrats and Republicans are not motivated to change our current system, which makes dominance of the two parties all but certain. It will be up to courageous candidates who are neither Republican nor Democrat, along with the U.S. electorate, to change the distribution of seats.

It is critical for a third party that can provide the platform for a candidate like Pat to emerge. There are dozens of ideas on how to change our system, but unfortunately, all of them would ultimately need the legislators to approve the changes. And they have absolutely no incentive to do that now. They get elected to their powerful positions by their core constituencies, who are truly the only people represented at the federal level.

The middle is up against it, no question. But there is a way to make a change which would allow a candidate like Pat to have a chance to be heard loud and clear by the electorate. That plan – which does not require a billionaire sugar daddy or sugar momma – follows in the next chapter.

The '15-5' plan for electoral change

In a political system configured to keep the Republicans and Democrats in power for perpetuity, our candidate Pat faces a tremendous uphill struggle. The legislators in office have absolutely no incentive to make changes in the financing of presidential campaigns. The only way it will ever change is if the electorate makes the sitting members of Congress feel their seats are in jeopardy.

But change is not impossible. In our democracy, if enough people decide they have had enough of post-truth politics, they can speak as a group that will make a difference.

For Pat and like-minded individuals who believe it's time for an end to the system that results in our two major political parties nominating candidates like Donald Trump and Hillary Clinton, here is the blueprint to create change:

1. Dedication to truth

Pat must have the personality traits and integrity described in the earlier personality profile. At the top of the list must be the commitment to tell the truth. Without this, everything from this point would be either a wasted effort or would morph into a splinter group from one of the two primary parties. Our electorate must have the choice of a candidate who stands on the moral high ground. This is the only way we can know for sure if there is truly a chance to reverse the U.S. political culture.

There is a chance we are already too far down the moral abyss, and therefore Pat's leadership is needed. Without it, the country as we used to know it will eventually cease to exist.

Pat will need a core group of supporters who will be able to start what is best described as a grass-roots campaign, with some very modern twists. One of the tasks of the supporters will be to create a simple but definitive slogan that says, "I won't lie." More importantly, Pat must do as he or she says. Lies or political-speak will immediately ruin the reputation Pat will need to establish.

Pat will need to have a personal background that contains little to no fodder for the mainstream and social media. No candidate will avoid the media surge of "vetting," but providing as little "dirt" as possible will prove to be important moving ahead.

2. Social media grass roots

Pat's core group of supporters will need to include one or more people with an understanding of social media marketing. A website will be necessary, as will a plan coordinating the use of Facebook, Twitter, and LinkedIn. The starting point is gaining membership in Facebook and LinkedIn groups of like-minded people who are tired of outright lying and corruption at the presidential level.

This was a method the "fake news" distributors of the 2016 campaign used with great success – relying on members of these groups to like and share the stories because of their delight in and-or passion for the topic or message. This is not to suggest Pat and company should try anything nefarious or dishonest. Just allow social media to perform its most innate function – spreading the word.

The social media campaign would include a Facebook page and group where people who are enamored of Pat's ideas could like or join. Then Pat's messages can get wider distribution on a regular basis than by releasing information in the like-minded groups alone.

The awareness portion of the campaign will need to begin years before the actual election, much like candidates from the legacy parties must do. Name recognition is a major factor in any election, and it can't begin early enough.

3. Decide on which party's ticket to run

We've outlined in this book the reasons why a candidate like Pat is not a good fit for either the Democratic or Republican ticket. One of the best reasons is there are already Congress members, Senators and celebrities who are laying the groundwork for a 2020 run for president in both parties. Pat is not going to have the resources or name recognition to have a chance in a primary election in which only Democrats or only Republicans are voting. You must be within the machine to emerge from it. The people in the Democratic and Republican machines have been in them for decades.

Other options? If Pat wants to start completely from scratch, he or she could start a new political party. But the odds on that strategy being successful anytime soon would be very slim.

The requirements for recognition of a new political party vary from state to state. In some states, a party may have to file a petition to qualify for ballot placement. In other states, a party must organize around a candidate for a particular office; that candidate must, in turn, win a percentage of the vote for the party to receive ballot status. In still other states, an aspiring political party must register a certain number of voters.

For example, here are the requirements for Louisiana:

> 1) there are at least 1,000 registered voters in the state registered as being affiliated with such party;
>
> 2) the political party has filed a notarized political party registration statement with the secretary of state; and
>
> 3) the political party has paid a registration fee of $1,000 to the secretary of state.

In California, the process outlined on the Secretary of State's website is nearly 1,500 words. The primary components of the description are:

Beginning the Process of Qualifying a Political Party

Whenever a group of electors desires to qualify a new political party, the group shall form a political body by carrying out the following two requirements (Elections Code § 5001):

• Hold a Caucus or Convention

• Filing Notice with Secretary of State

Two Methods to Qualify a Political Party

Voter Registration Method - Elections Code Section 5100(b) or 5151(c)

To qualify a new political party by voter registration requires that voters equal in number to at least 0.33 percent of the total number of voters registered on the 154th day before the primary election or the 123rd day before the presidential general election complete an affidavit of registration, disclosing a preference by writing in the name of the political body intending to qualify as a political party. (Elections Code §§ 5100(b), 5151(c).) ...

Petition Method - Elections Code Section 5100(c) or 5151(d)

To qualify a new political party by petition, no later than 135 days prior to the primary election or the presidential general election, the Secretary of State must determine if a political body intending to qualify collected petition signatures of registered voters equal to 10 percent of the votes cast at the last gubernatorial election. (Elections Code §§ 5100(c), 5151(d).) The current signature requirement is 751,398 (10% of 7,513,972, the votes cast at the November 4, 2014, gubernatorial election). ...

Imagine Pat and his-her small core of supporters trying to meet all the requirements of each of the 50 states. (Keep in mind we presented a very small portion of California's requirements.) A strategy more likely to be successful would be to run as a candidate for an existing party already registered and recognized within every state ... like the Libertarian Party.

The party's website in early 2017 had the following description:[45]

The Libertarian Party (LP) is your representative in American politics. It is the only political organization which respects you as a unique and responsible individual.

Our slogan is that we are "The Party of Principle," because we stand firmly on our principles.

Libertarians strongly oppose any government interference into their personal, family, and business decisions. Essentially, we believe all

Americans should be free to live their lives and pursue their interests as they see fit as long as they do no harm to another.

Founded in 1971, we run many hundred (sic) of candidates every election cycle. These candidates seek positions ranging from City Council to President of the United States. Each of these candidates helps to give liberty a voice.

THE LIBERTARIAN OPTION

• Consider voting Libertarian or joining the Libertarian Party because...

• We seek to substantially reduce the size and intrusiveness of government and cut and eliminate taxes at every opportunity.

• We believe that peaceful, honest people should be able to offer their goods and services to willing consumers without inappropriate interference from government.

• We believe that peaceful, honest people should decide for themselves how to live their lives, without fear of criminal or civil penalties.

• We believe that government's only responsibility, if any, should be protecting people from force and fraud.

Pat will need to decide if these position statements fit him or her as a person. Presuming so, the process could continue.

4. Getting on the ballot

This is the point when the social media campaign must gear up considerably. It must incorporate paid advertising on Facebook and must engage the use of social media "bots."

A social "bot" is a software program that simulates human behavior in automated interactions on social network sites such as Facebook and Twitter.

As a rule, social bots are sophisticated enough to fool other users and be taken for a human. To do so, social bots use artificial intelligence (AI), text mining and data analysis software. Some have access to databases of general knowledge information and current events to allow them to recognize references and craft more convincing messages.

Social bots are usually programmed to interact as a human does, following relatively normal sleep/wake cycles and sending messages on a somewhat randomized schedule rather than at regular intervals. Twitter is the most common platform for social bots because the microblogging format is well-suited to the software's capabilities.

Most social bots get created for a specific purpose, such as marketing, political campaigning or public relations. In March 2017, the news program 60 Minutes presented a report on just how social bots were used to boost the social media rank of fake news during the 2016 presidential campaign. A transcribed portion of that report appears here:[46]

Scott Pelley: So when we're talking about these bots, these are Twitter accounts masquerading as real people.

Jim Vidmar, an Internet consultant: That's right.

Pelley: By the thousands?

Vidmar: By the millions.

CBS did an experiment with Vidmar's help. The network bought 5,000 bots from a Russian website—they cost just a few hundred bucks.

Pelley: We've set up an experiment so you can show me how this works. And I'm going to tweet from my account, "What happens when 60 Minutes investigates fake news?" So tweet that out.

Normally, Pelley said, he could expect real people to retweet his message a few dozen times. Vidmar programmed the bots to retweet Pelley's message and then turned them loose.

Pelley: Hit it with everything you've got.

Vidmar: Let's hit it with everything we got. ... There you go. Now you've got 3.2 thousand retweets right there.

Pelley: Wait a minute. I went from 300 to 3,000?

Vidmar: Now, it's 4.4 thousand. … Now real people start seeing it. They start retweeting it, and, you know, responding to it.

Pelley: And it takes off.

Vidmar: And it takes off.

This matters because Facebook and Twitter select articles to present prominently based mostly on how popular they are, and bots can fool the two social media titans. CBS's bots expanded the reach of its message 9,000 percent.

There is nothing illegal at this point about utilizing bots. It is a way to emerge from the din of millions of other posts and tweets. There would have been no consternation about their use in 2016 if the news articles and posts they boosted were all factually correct. If Pat's campaign remains on message and truthful, there should be no political price to pay for this strategy.

And, if Pat is asked whether bots are being utilized in the campaign, the honest response would be, "Yes. We are using advanced marketing strategies that all serious marketers have at least considered at one time or another. The other campaigns are probably using them, as well, though I can't verify that for sure."

In most states, getting on the presidential primary ballot consists of securing the signatures of a specified number of registered voters, representing a percentage of those who voted in the previous presidential election. Paying a filing fee may also apply. These fees could total well over $100,000 over the 50 states.

But not for the Libertarian Party! The Libertarian nominee for president gets selected at the party's national convention. Libertarians from the 50 states and District of Columbia meet in Orlando in May. In 2016, 1,047 delegates were selected to attend the Libertarian National Convention. The number varies because delegates get selected at each state's Libertarian convention. While each state has a quota, there is no guarantee that each state will find enough people motivated to participate and attend to fill all its delegate seats. Delegates are not required to go to the national convention committed to any one candidate, although some certainly are because of previous relationships and interactions.

To be nominated, a candidate must have the written support of 30 delegates to the convention — no delegate may nominate more than one individual.[47] This would obviously require some lobbying by Pat and supporters, which is why the social media campaign must already be under way. If it is evident there is a substantial public awareness and support of Pat and his-her platform, it will be much easier to appeal to delegates of a party which may see Pat as a catalyst for more acceptance and awareness.

In the second round of delegate voting, the candidate with the fewest votes, and any candidate that has failed to receive five percent of the votes, is left off the ballot. That same process continues for all subsequent rounds until a candidate receives a majority.

The fly in the ointment for Pat is that the delegates to the national convention are not committed to a specific candidate. Voting in state primaries has no binding effect. All sorts of political wheeling and dealing can take place. The Libertarian option is the path of least resistance among parties registered to appear on the ballots in all 50 states. But if 30 delegates can't be persuaded to nominate Pat in writing, then the effort dies there.

Another option is running completely independent. It is possible for someone with gargantuan grass-roots support. Ballotpedia.org estimated that approximately 884,000 valid signatures of registered voters would have needed to be collected across the country for an independent to appear on the ballot in all 50 states in 2016.[48] The requirements are different from state to state, with the required number representing between 1 and 5 percent of votes cast in the most recent statewide or presidential election.

The estimates for required signatures from Ballotpedia were as high as 187,000 for inclusion on the California ballot, to as low as 275 in Tennessee. Thirty-six of the 50 states (and the District of Columbia) required 10,000 signatures or fewer in 2016, according to Ballotpedia. The states over that mark, along with California, were Arizona, Florida, Illinois, Indiana, Maryland, Michigan, New Mexico, New York, North Carolina, Oklahoma, Oregon, Pennsylvania and Texas.

The plan proposed here is a long-term plan designed to span at least two presidential campaign cycles. It would be great to think that Pat could disrupt the entire U.S. political system as an independent in one election, but it is highly unlikely. The goal initially is to get on as many states' ballots as possible. An independent run without the 14 states that require more than 10,000 signatures has close to zero percent chance of an electoral college victory scenario.

The chances of Pat being taken seriously without an actual scenario for victory would also be near zero. Therefore, the

Libertarian ballot scenario is the path of least resistance with the opportunity for victories in every state.

5. Participation by voters in the "middle"

Having reached this point – appearance on presidential ballots – is an amazing accomplishment. Now Pat needs the support of the 40 percent or so of the electorate who consider themselves independent.

These "middle" voters must reject the mantra of "voting for a third-party candidate is essentially casting a vote for (insert your Democratic or Republican candidate of choice here)." No voter should ever believe that voting his or her choice is a wasted vote – now more than ever.

When televised presidential debates start, the Democratic and Republican nominees are guaranteed a spot on the stage. How does an independent or third-party candidate gain inclusion? He or she must achieve at least 15 percent support among the national electorate in public opinion polling.

This threshold is set by the Commission on Presidential Debates. To participate in the debates, candidates need "support of at least 15 percent of the national electorate as determined by five selected national public opinion polling organizations, using the average of those organizations' most recently publicly reported results at the time of the determination."

This is the chance for the voters in the middle, who are represented by basically nobody in either major political party, to make themselves heard.

You may remember the Dr. Seuss classic book, "Horton Hears a Who." Horton the elephant could hear, with his large ears, the voices of microscopic persons known as "Whos" living on a dust speck. But he was shunned and taunted by animals around him in the jungle who could not hear them. Horton's jungle neighbors thought he was lying.

An unruly mob of doubting animals decided to boil the dust speck to end what they saw as Horton's false claims. But Horton persuaded every member of the Who society to cry out, "We are here!" Their combined volume made their voices audible to the other animals, which stopped the effort to boil the dust speck and led to recognition by the masses.

When polling organizations, or even friends and relatives, ask which candidate the "middle" electorate will support in 2020, the "middle" voter should confidently answer, "Pat." That will be the middle voters' equivalent of yelling, "We are here!" This is the key to getting Pat on stage with the two legacy party candidates. This opportunity for voters to compare them side by side, and to hear how their responses vary, increases Pat's chances by an unmeasurable number.

What it says to the entire electorate is that there are enough voters out there who support Pat that he-she could earn a place on the stage to debate the issues and other candidates. It's more than a token candidacy. A vote cast for Pat will be a vote that counts and can make a difference.

6. The "15-5 Plan"

Participating in televised debates watched by tens of millions gave the Texas billionaire Ross Perot the legitimacy and visibility to get 20 percent of the vote in 1992. This leads us to the second component of our "15-5 Plan for Pat:"

The 15 (or more) percent of support among people polled got Pat on the debate stage. The 5 represents the percentage of popular votes nationwide that Pat would need to gather to qualify for public funding for the Libertarian Party in the next presidential election cycle. In 2016, that would have resulted in a grant of tens of millions of dollars to be used for campaigning.

The legacy party candidates did not accept the grants because what they received from private donors far exceeded what would have been a $91 million grant for both Democrats and Republicans. One caveat of the grant is that the recipient candidate cannot raise funds from outside sources.

In Pat's case, the tens of millions would likely more than cover all the very basic costs of the next presidential campaign cycle. Along with increased name recognition, the funding would give Pat the chance to run as much more of a political equal in 2024 than in 2020. The grants are subject to cost of living increases, so they will very likely be close to or exceed $100 million by 2020.

You can help in this effort by checking yes for the "Do you want $3 of your federal tax to go to the Presidential Election Campaign Fund?" question on your federal income tax form. Checking yes does not increase the amount of tax you pay. It merely places $3 of the tax you paid into the Presidential Election Campaign Fund, the source of the grants. Every person who checks yes will mean that much more in the fund available for Pat's use in 2020. (The Democrats and Republicans won't be drawing from this funding source.)

You may have been hoping for a quick and easy plan that would have meant immediate change and victory for Pat. It may be out there. If so, we encourage you to share your ideas and feedback at fixposttruthpolitics.com, to instigate additional brainstorming and discussion. We tried to look at this scenario as realistically as possible, considering the level of entrenchment of the Republicans, Democrats and their political machines.

This timeline also accounts for the lack of meaningful involvement in the political process by a significant percentage of Americans. Only about 57 percent of voting-age Americans cast ballots in the 2016 election, which was the lowest turnout in 20 years. It's quite clear that disillusionment and even disgust with our electoral system – capped off by the nomination of two clearly unfit candidates in 2016 – is a factor.

It's going to take at least one full cycle for enough people to believe that such a radical change is possible to make an actual difference, and to get them to either re-engage or engage for the first time. The devoted members of the legacy political parties will always vote for their ticket. It is the currently unrepresented and largely disgusted political middle that holds the key to Pat's success.

As mentioned early in the book, a significant percentage of people who voted in 2016 did not cast a vote for president, apparently due to their dissatisfaction in their choices. A much larger percentage of people voted for what they perceived as the lesser of two evils, instead of someone who they felt good about.

CNN exit polling showed only 38 percent of voters who went to the polls had a favorable view of Donald Trump. The same minority percentage of people leaving the polls told CNN they thought Trump was qualified to be president. Only one in three said they thought he was "honest and trustworthy." Yet, a candidate with these terrible exit polling numbers won the election. The only possible conclusion is that voters thought they had two terrible choices and picked the one they thought was the lesser evil. This is absolutely no way for a country like the United States to proceed politically.

Billionaire Mark Cuban called it "political chemotherapy" in an interview with CNN. He described a friend who described why he voted for Trump.

"I voted for politicians my entire life," Cuban said in quoting his friend, whose name he did not disclose. "Do you know what the definition of insanity is? Doing the same thing over and over and expecting (different) results. So I voted for Donald Trump. Is he poisonous in a lot of respects? Yeah. He's our chemotherapy. We hope he's going to change the political system."

Indeed, the CNN exit polling numbers showed that 39 percent of voters said the most important character trait for a candidate was that he or she "can bring change." Trump won that group, 82 percent to 14 percent.[49] Clearly our nation is thirsty for change, but not the kind of change that Trump offers.

If Pat does not step forward, and the members of the electorate who think independently do not engage in the political process, the United States' future as a thriving society and leader on the world stage is in great jeopardy.

We can't have post-truth politics as our modus operandi. What happens when a president we don't trust tells us we need to go to war? Will he or she have cried wolf too many times? Will anyone believe that a habitual liar has anything but his or her own best interests in mind? At times like that, or other great crises, our country needs a leader.

If the first thing you as a citizen think of when you hear the elected leader of your country speak is, "I wonder if it's another lie?", there is a big problem. And there is.

We've created a website where you can express your thoughts on these issues, and engage in discussion with others who have similar concerns.[50] Between this book and the ideas gleaned from our website, the hope is Pat will be made aware of the options available to him or her in a run for the presidency. And, we hope the largely unengaged political middle will recognize that they are the only hope for real change in our completely broken political system.

Members of the two legacy parties are smugly smiling and giving a slight affirmative nod, as if to say, best of luck to you. In their minds, this idea has no chance of working. And you really can't blame them for their cockiness. The most effective third-party candidate of the past half-century was Ross Perot, and he was still 20 to 25 percent away from chance for a victory.

You may believe one or both of the legacy parties will see the need to nominate someone like Pat, so the Herculean effort to get Pat on the ballot may not be necessary. That is pure wishful thinking. The Democratic nominee in 2020 is going to be someone who can be more theatric than Donald Trump. The Democratic base will demand it. And the Democratic base will get what it wants, right, Bernie Sanders?

Pat's efforts to get on the ballot are only half of the equation needed to fix post-truth politics. The other necessary component is the willingness of the voters in the middle – independents and those on the fringes of the Democratic and Republican parties – to vote their beliefs. If Pat is the person you believe is the best choice, don't let people tell you that a vote for Pat is really a vote for Donald Trump or whichever candidate the Democrats nominate.

Failure to act on your beliefs will result in the post-truth political era becoming further entrenched. If you believe post-truth politics do not represent you, members of the "middle" plurality must stop conceding political control to the GOP and Dems.

Express yourself:
Tell us what you think

Visit http://fixposttruthpolitics.com
- **Join our online discussions**
- **Follow latest news on this topic**

Email: admin@fixposttruthpolitics.com
- **Suggest discussion and post topics**
- **Keep us posted on anything happening that relates to the content of this book**

Like us on social media:
- **Facebook:** https://www.facebook.com/fixposttruthpolitics/
- **Twitter:** https://twitter.com/posttruthpoliti
- **Pinterest:** https://www.pinterest.com/tmitsoff/fixing-post-truth-politics/

About the author

Tom Mitsoff is an award-winning journalist and writer whose 30-year career was focused in the newspaper industry. In his roles as a managing editor, editor-in-chief and executive editor and co-owner of daily and weekly newspapers, he had a front-row seat for the transformations of newspapers and other mass media over the past three decades as described in this book.

Tom has more than 1,000 bylined articles in printed publications, and has served as the editor in charge of more than 2,000 issues of news publications. He also ran the online news websites for three daily and weekly newspaper companies for 15 years.

Endnotes

[1] http://bestseller.posttruthbook.com
[2] http://blog.wfmu.org/freeform/2010/09/richard-nixons-laugh-in.html
[3] http://time.com/4292027/gerald-ford-saturday-night-live/
[4] https://www.calcable.org/learn/history-of-cable/
[5] https://www.calcable.org/learn/history-of-cable/
[6] http://www.npr.org/2014/07/30/336538635/former-cnn-anchor-bernard-shaw-kept-cool-but-paid-the-price-of-success
[7] https://www.calcable.org/learn/history-of-cable/
[8] https://www.calcable.org/learn/history-of-cable/
[9]

http://www.drudgereportarchives.com/data/2002/01/17/20020117_175502_ml.htm
[10] http://www.gallup.com/poll/195542/americans-trust-mass-media-sinks-new-low.aspx
[11] https://wikileaks.org/podesta-emails/emailid/38478
[12] http://www.politico.com/blogs/media/2015/05/george-stephanopoulos-discloses-75-000-contribution-to-clinton-foundation-207120
[13] http://www.politico.com/blogs/on-media/2016/11/fox-news-bret-baier-sorry-for-clinton-foundation-report-230743
[14] https://www.spj.org/ethics-papers-anonymity.asp
[15] https://medium.com/@dicktofel/the-sky-is-falling-on-print-newspapers-faster-than-you-think-c84a2f9a9df4
[16] http://computer.howstuffworks.com/web-advertising2.htm
[17] http://www.crainsdetroit.com/article/20161115/NEWS/161119862/detroit-news-offers-buyouts-to-all-editorial-employees
[18] http://www.crainsdetroit.com/article/20161216/NEWS/161219863/detroit-news-cuts-finance-columnist-editors-photo-staffers
[19] https://allora.io/websites-using/taboola/
[20] https://www.taboola.com/press-release/media-advisory-experience-world%E2%80%99s-leading-content-discovery-platform-taboola-ces-2015

[21] http://gutenberg.us/articles/eng/Selective_exposure_theory

[22] http://www.dartmouth.edu/~seanjwestwood/papers/CRsocialNews.pdf

[23] https://www.buzzfeed.com/craigsilverman/how-macedonia-became-a-global-hub-for-pro-trump-misinfo?utm_term=.agAQpbpoK#.dt8rjVjNR

[24] https://www.washingtonpost.com/business/economy/russian-propaganda-effort-helped-spread-fake-news-during-election-experts-say/2016/11/24/793903b6-8a40-4ca9-b712-716af66098fe_story.html?utm_term=.c3e829076e7d

[25] http://www.marketwatch.com/story/this-person-makes-10000-a-month-writing-fake-news-2016-11-17

[26] http://abcnews.com.co/obama-signs-executive-order-declaring-investigation-of-election-results/

[27] https://www.washingtonpost.com/news/the-intersect/wp/2016/11/17/facebook-fake-news-writer-i-think-donald-trump-is-in-the-white-house-because-of-me/?utm_term=.00adccb89973

[28] https://newsroom.fb.com/news/2016/12/news-feed-fyi-addressing-hoaxes-and-fake-news/

[29] http://www.niemanlab.org/2016/05/pew-report-44-percent-of-u-s-adults-get-news-on-facebook/

[30] http://ijr.com/opinion/2016/11/261600-hillary-clinton-lies-top/

[31] http://www.rightwingwatch.org/post/101-donald-trump-lies-the-gop-presidential-nominees-pathological-dishonesty/

[32] http://www.npr.org/2016/02/28/467961962/sick-of-political-parties-unaffiliated-voters-are-changing-politics

[33] http://www.latimes.com/opinion/op-ed/la-oe-david-french-president-bill-kristol-20160601-snap-story.html

[34] http://www.chicagotribune.com/news/opinion/commentary/ct-hillary-clinton-donald-trump-ted-cruz-20160404-story.html

[35] https://www.bloomberg.com/politics/graphics/2016-presidential-campaign-fundraising/

[36] https://www.opensecrets.org/outsidespending/summ.php?chrt=V&type=S

[37] https://www.amazon.com/Golden-Rule-Investment-Competition-Money-Driven/dp/0226243176

[38] http://time.com/4436805/lawrence-lessig-randy-barnett/

[39] https://www.betterforamerica.com/for_immediate_release

[40] https://ballotpedia.org/History_of_Donald_Trump%27s_political_donations

[41] https://thinkprogress.org/the-288-million-in-campaign-funds-that-candidates-arent-using-fa62673bbcdc

[42] http://www.cambridgeblog.org/2016/01/sorted-polarized-and-gridlocked-in-2016/

[43] https://www.washingtonpost.com/news/monkey-cage/wp/2014/01/21/americans-arent-polarized-just-better-sorted/?utm_term=.07770c2acf7f

[44] http://www.gallup.com/poll/180440/new-record-political-independents.aspx

[45] https://www.lp.org/about/
[46] http://www.cbsnews.com/news/how-fake-news-find-your-social-media-feeds/
[47] https://www.conservativereview.com/commentary/2016/05/6-things-you-should-know-about-the-libertarian-party
[48]

https://ballotpedia.org/Filing_deadlines_and_signature_requirements_for_independent_presidential_candidates,_2016
[49] http://www.cnn.com/2017/04/21/politics/mark-cuban-donald-trump/index.html
[50] http://www.fixposttruthpolitics.com

www.ingramcontent.com/pod-product-compliance
Lightning Source LLC
Chambersburg PA
CBHW050133280326
41933CB00010B/1359